PAUL
THE APOSTLE

Jew, Tarsian, Roman

W. H. BOULTON

THE CHRISTADELPHIAN,
404 SHAFTMOOR LANE,
BIRMINGHAM B28 8SZ

1984

Second edition 1956
Reprinted 1971, 1977
Third edition 1984

ISBN 0 85189 0415

PRINTED IN GREAT BRITAIN BY OFFSET LITHOGRAPHY BY
BILLING & SONS LTD, WORCESTER

CONTENTS

iii.

ILLUSTRATIONS AND MAPS

Cover: MILETUS: View of Quay from Theatre (L.H.)
"A great door . . . is opened unto me" (1 Cor. 16:9)

Acknowledgements: Sources are acknowledged, where appropriate, in the captions. We are particularly indebted to Christadelphian brethren for their help: N. E. Hughes for maps drawn for the previous edition; Tom Barling, Maurice Fry, Lionel Haines and Doug Hardy for the loan of colour transparencies (indicated by initials in the list above).

iv.

PREFACE

ALTHOUGH this is the third time the Author has tried to picture the life of Saul of Tarsus—once in the pages of *The Christadelphian*, and, later, in book form—this is not in any way a revision of either of these past attempts. A close comparison may show certain passages reproduced from the earlier presentations, but as a whole it is a new book, issued with a new purpose. Paul once wrote, " Be ye imitators of me, even as I also am of Christ ", and if this attempt to picture his life leads any one to imitate him, it will have achieved its object.

April, 1946

NOTE TO THE 1984 EDITION

THE TEXT has been reprinted unchanged, but the rather dated photographs have been replaced by a new selection of black and white illustrations and colour plates. We trust these will be found attractive and helpful.

A FOREWORD

THIS is the story of a man who, eleven years before he met his death at the hands of a Roman executioner, was able to say of himself that he had been

> In labours more abundantly,
> In stripes above measure,
> In prisons more frequently,
> In deaths oft.

> Of the Jews five times received I forty stripes save one.
> Thrice was I beaten with rods,
> Once was I stoned.
> Thrice I suffered shipwreck,
> A night and a day have I been in the deep.

> In journeyings often,
> In perils of rivers,
> In perils of robbers,
> In perils from my countrymen,
> In perils from the Gentiles,
> In perils in the city,
> In perils in the wilderness,
> In perils in the sea,
> In perils among false brethren.

> In labour and travail,
> In watchings often,
> In hunger and thirst,
> In fastings often,
> In cold and nakedness.

Then, as if this were not enough for one man to endure, he added a further item, " Anxiety for all the churches ".

Although many of the things thus mentioned find no place in the record of his life, those that are referred to are enough to justify one more attempt to tell his life once again. If any further reason is needed, it will be found in a saying of one who has written of him, " he was the greatest human being that ever followed Jesus Christ ".

CHAPTER I

A JEW OF TARSUS

ABOUT the year 1 of the Christian Era a boy was
born to Jewish parents in Tarsus, the chief city
of Cilicia, where the family seems to have been
established for a long time. Four or five years
earlier another boy had been born in Bethlehem
of Judea. In those days no one would have
ventured to suggest that there would have been
any connection between the two boys, yet it was
destined that they should occupy the relationship
of servant and Master. In his later years Saul,
the boy of Tarsus, often spoke of himself as the
servant, or more correctly, the slave, of Jesus,
the boy of Bethlehem.

The work that Saul was to do was a great
one, and called for much preparation. Many
things, including even the experiences of his
boyhood in Tarsus, contributed to this preparation.

Tarsus was a city of repute, old established
when Saul was born ; he himself described it,
in after years, as " no mean city ". Some of its
importance was due to its geographical position,
some to the activities of its citizens. It stood on
the river Cydnus, which wound its way through
a wide and fertile plain from the Taurus Mountains to the Mediterranean Sea. It was connected with a system of roads leading in various

directions. At some time in the past the Tarsians had constructed a road from their city to what were known as the Cilician Gates, a pass through the Taurus Mountains, thus giving access to the central parts of Asia Minor and to Ephesus, from which sea routes led to Athens, to Corinth, and to Rome.

Being on the navigable portion of the River Cydnus, Tarsus was a port, and in its docks and warehouses home and foreign produce passed, bringing much wealth to its inhabitants. Ships from many lands came into its port, and men of various races walked through its streets. Though the boy Saul was a Jew, he must often have noted, and probably talked to, these strangers who trod the ways of the district, and the things he saw and heard had a place in forming his mind, and preparing him for the work he was destined to do.

Tarsus was also a place of learning, and a seat of Greek culture ; it possessed a famous university where the youth of the city and the surrounding districts could obtain a good education. Its scholars travelled far and wide, and though Strabo, the Greek historian, says that few of them returned home, they exercised a considerable influence on the thought and culture of the times. It is doubtful whether Saul received any of his education at the university of Tarsus, though from the way in which he occasionally quoted from Gentile poets he certainly came into contact with some who did.

Of his family little is known. It consisted of at least four persons, his father, his mother, a sister, and himself. Both parents were Jews, for he once described himself as " a Hebrew of Hebrews ". They were of the tribe of Benjamin and his name may have been given to him because it was the name of Israel's first king, who also was a Benjamite.

Nothing is recorded of the earlier history of the family, but it may be assumed that they were of good standing in the city. The father was a citizen, and the citizenship did not pertain to any one because he happened to be born there. Probably the family had been established in the city since the days when a Syrian king, Antiochus Epiphanes, caused a number of Jewish families to settle in Asia Minor. If that assumption is correct the family must have been in Cilicia about a hundred and fifty years.

Saul's father possessed a dignity that was to stand the son in good stead in later years. About a hundred years before, Cilicia had become a Roman province, and Roman citizenship was conferred on a number of its inhabitants, and some ancestor may have obtained the citizenship then. A Roman citizen occupied a position of importance in a provincial town.

Each of the matters that have been mentioned had an influence upon Saul as he grew up ; they taught him that he was a Jew, a Tarsian, and a Roman. There was one other fact, however, that had a great influence upon him, and helped to shape his destiny ; he was the son of a Pharisee. On a man such as Saul grew up to be, the religious outlook on life is the most important of all.

A conscientious Pharisee, as Saul's father must have been, held firmly to the teachings of the Mosaic Law, as explained by the traditions of the elders, as they were called. A Pharisee living among the Greek population of Asia Minor must not be judged by the Pharisees of Jerusalem who so bitterly opposed Jesus of Nazareth. Originally the Pharisees stood for purity in religion, both as regards belief and practice, and though they became a self-righteous community, even in Jerusalem they included such men as Nicodemus and Joseph of Arimathea. Saul's father probably belonged to the better type of the Pharisees.

One of the most important things in a boy's life is his education. It may be assumed that Saul's early tuition was carried on in accordance with the provisions of the Mosaic Law. Foremost among these was the one which said, " Hear, O Israel, the Lord our God is one Lord : and thou shalt love the Lord thy God with all thine heart, and with all thy soul, and with all thy might. And these words which I command thee this day, shall be upon thine heart : and thou shalt teach them diligently unto thy children ". Those " words " would be repeated to the young Saul by his father and mother ; they would

4

include the laws, the statutes, and the judgments given by Moses to the people of Israel. The case of Timothy may be taken as an illustration of this phase of the education given to a Jewish boy living in a Gentile community. Of Timothy it is said " From a babe thou hast known the sacred writings which are able to make thee wise unto salvation ". If that were the case with Timothy, whose father was a Gentile, it must have been true of Saul, whose father was a Pharisee. No doubt there was a Jewish school in Tarsus, where Saul's home training would be supplemented by tuition of a more systematic character.

Both at home and at school Saul would be taught to repeat sections of the Holy Scriptures, and would be told of the doings of his people in the brave days of old. In this way his mind became stored with memories of incidents in the life of Abraham ; of the great deliverance of his ancestors from Egypt ; of Joshua conquering the land promised to the fathers. He would learn of the shepherd boy who became musician, soldier, outlaw, and king, and his eyes must have sparkled as he heard for the first time of the fight between David and Goliath. Solomon's glory would appeal to him in another way. The story of Hezekiah, Isaiah, and Sennacherib would hold him spellbound. He would sympathize with Jeremiah ; sorrow over the fall of Judah ; and sigh with the exiles who could not sing the Lord's song in a strange land. He would learn of Ezra and Nehemiah, and his heart must have swelled at the recital of the deeds of the Maccabees.

One thing more he would have learned in those early years, the promise of a coming Redeemer, a great One who would restore Israel, be the glory of his people, and a Light to lighten the Gentiles.

By these combined influences—his strict Jewish home training, and his experiences in a Greek city—Saul's mind was being prepared for his future career. No one could have foretold what result such differing influences would have on his impressionable mind, but we can see now that they were just what were required to fit him for the great work he was to do. One set of influences made him acquainted with the ways of Greek life, and furnished him with many of the illustrations which he used in his later life ; especially in his letters—combats in the arena ; the strenuous efforts of those who ran in a race ; the ways of the athlete ; the hard-hitting of the boxer. He may, or may not, have witnessed these things ; the Pharisaic influence of his Jewish home may have kept him from them, but he would certainly hear them spoken of by other boys, and the natural curiosity of the opening mind of a lad like Saul may have caused him to see them. Altogether things combined to give a Grecian background to his Jewish thoughts.

Above all, the principal influence of those early years of home and school life gave him a great familiarity with the Hebrew Scriptures. One has only to read his addresses, or his letters, to see how much at home he was in them. No amount of desultory reading could have given him his remarkable facility of applying them to the matters of which he spoke and wrote.

At the age of twelve it was customary for a Jewish lad to be taught a trade. Three things were enjoined on Jewish fathers who had sons. They must be circumcised; they must be taught the Law; and they must be taught a trade. One rabbi said, " Whosoever does not teach his son a trade is as if he brought him up to be a robber ". They also said a son should be taught the trade of his father, so that Saul's father may have been a cloth merchant. Saul's trade may have been partly decided on by the situation of Tarsus. Cilicia was noted for its goats, from the long hair of which a cloth was woven which was particularly suitable for tent-making. The trade was a poorly paid one, and would provide little for Saul's wants in after days when his hands had to minister to his necessities.

At the same time cloth-making was a mechanical process which left the mind free. In this there is another indication of a divine providence that overruled the affairs of Saul's early days, preparing him for his future work.

Thus in these early years a threefold preparation, and three leading influences, may be discerned; Jewish, Greek, and Roman. The first gave him a pride of race and a profound knowledge of the Oracles of God. The second developed in him a quickness of apprehension, and a skill in argument ; and the third, the solidity of Rome and its institutions—his respect for law and order.

CHAPTER II

BROUGHT UP IN JERUSALEM

ALTHOUGH Saul was taught the arts of cloth-weaving and tent-making, his father had no intention that he should depend upon them for a living. Saul was a promising youngster, and his father had more ambitious designs for his future. His desire was that his son should become a rabbi, and thus occupy one of the most honourable positions to which a Jew could attain. It should however be borne in mind that most rabbis continued to carry on their trades in addition to their labours of teaching.

To gain admission into the ranks of the rabbis it was necessary for Saul to go to Jerusalem, for only there would it be possible for him to obtain the learning and the training that would qualify him for such a position. It must have meant a good deal for the father, and even more for the mother, to part with their son ; probably it meant just as much for his sister. Travel, though not unusual in those days, was not so simple as it is now, and Jerusalem was hundreds of miles away from Tarsus.

It is quite likely that Saul journeyed to Jerusalem with his father on the occasion of one of the great feasts, when hundreds of Jews who lived in Gentile lands made their way to the Holy City. They often travelled in companies, and Saul and his father probably joined one that went by sea to Caesarea, the great city that had been built by Herod the Great, and which had become the headquarters of Roman rule in Palestine. As they travelled these bands of pilgrims whiled away the time by singing some of the Songs of Zion, particularly those called the Songs of Ascents in the book of Psalms. The young Saul would join heartily as they sang :

Pray for the peace of Jerusalem ;
They shall prosper that love thee.
Peace be within thy walls,
And prosperity within thy palaces.

His voice would sound out enthusiastically as he joined in another :

They that trust in the Lord
Are as Mount Zion, which cannot be moved,
but abideth for ever.

As the mountains are round about Jerusalem,
So the Lord is round about His people,
From this time forth, and for evermore.

It was a great day in Saul's life when he first caught sight of the Holy City and the great Temple that Herod the Great had caused to be erected there. What were his thoughts as he entered through the gate of the city for the first time ? A thousand years had passed since it became the City of David. It had witnessed wonderful deliverances, and many reverses. Its streets had been trodden by men bearing the greatest names in Jewish history—and by some

10

of its worst. Its crowning glory was the Temple, and though the rabbis could say nothing good of its builder, they could not say enough of the building.

In those days there were two rabbinical schools in Jerusalem, those of Hillel and Schammai, doctors of the Law who had flourished some fifty years earlier. The principal difference between them was that the school of Hillel held that tradition was superior to the Law, whereas the other rejected tradition if it clashed with the Law. Gamaliel, who was the head of the school of Hillel, was his grandson, and the school with which he was associated was more influential than that of his rival. Though both schools existed for the same purpose, the training of rabbis, there were so many differences between them that it was popularly said that even Elijah would be unable to reconcile the disciples of the rival schools !

When the rabbi was teaching his pupils he usually sat on a chair, and the scholars sat round him on forms or on the ground. A passage from the Scriptures was read in Hebrew and translated into Aramaic, the every day language of Palestine. Definitions and interpretations were given ; allegories were suggested, and the opinions of various doctors of the Law were quoted and discussed. Legal enactments were examined as carefully as a modern lawyer analyses the terms of an Act of Parliament, weighing each word to get at the meaning of a clause. The historical portions of

11

the Scripture were treated more freely. The students listened, or enquired, just as the child Jesus had done on his visit to Jerusalem at the age of twelve.

Saul entered the school of Gamaliel where he was an exemplary pupil, and by the time he had finished his course he was ready to take up his life's work. By that time he had an intimate knowledge of the Law ; was conversant with the traditions ; he had a zeal for both far beyond the average student at a rabbinical school. So strict was he in his obedience to the Law that he could say that " as touching the righteousness which is in the Law (he was) blameless ".

Fortunately there was another side to the influence of Gamaliel. Though a Pharisee, he was not prejudiced against the learning of the Greeks ; he belonged to what, in modern times, would be called the liberal school of theology. Perhaps unnoticed by him, this influence affected Saul, and, though he gave no indication of it in the early part of his life, it stood him in good stead when he received his commission to preach the gospel of Christ to Jews and Greeks, Romans and barbarians.

Gamaliel was also a man of moderation. He saved the apostles when they were arraigned before the priests. " Take heed ", he said to the council, " refrain from these men and let them alone ; for if this counsel or this work be of men it will be overthrown ; but if it is of God ye will not be able to overthrow them, lest haply ye be found even to be fighting against God ".

Saul probably heard of this advice, and, coming from Gamaliel, it must have given him food for thought. He himself was convinced that all the agitation about Jesus of Nazareth ought to be put down, and yet here was the revered Gamaliel suggesting that it might be from God ! However, he was not going to listen to men like Peter and John, mere fishermen of Galilee ! The Law was his guide, and his boast.

At the end of his course of instruction Saul probably returned to Tarsus. No doubt he felt a glow of satisfaction at the difference in the attitude of his family and his friends towards him. He had gone away a mere lad ; he returned a rabbi. He possessed human feelings, and few men could experience such a change in the circumstances without being affected by it.

How long he remained in Tarsus is not known ; he was probably anxious to get back to Jerusalem ; that was where the great rabbis were to be found, and he wanted to be among them. It was probably during the time he was away from the holy city that the voice of Jesus of Nazareth had been heard in its streets. He had been received with cries of " Hosanna ", and acclaimed as the Son of David, the Messiah, though only a few days afterwards the cry was changed to " Crucify him ". When Saul returned he found the people perplexed by two contrary views that were being put forward

concerning Jesus. A number were boldly proclaiming that he had been raised from the dead
after his crucifixion, and that he was indeed the
Messiah. On the other hand there were those,
and they included the leaders of the people, the
Pharisees and the Sadducees, who stoutly main-
tained that he was dead, and that the whole thing
was a hoax. The former class was growing,
however, for " multitudes both of men and
women " were joining the sect of the Nazarenes ;
even a great company of the priests had done so.

Saul was a zealous Jew, a son of the Law,
an upholder of the traditions. These had been
given by God, and they must be upheld.
Whoever heard that the Messiah, for whose
coming he, like his fellows, longed, was to be
crucified, suffering the most ignominious death
it was possible to undergo ? Did not the Law
say, " He that is hanged is accursed of God " ?
No Messiah could undergo such an experience ;
it was incredible, so Saul cast in his lot with those
who were trying to put down the heresy. He
argued with some of the Nazarenes, but though
he was well grounded in the Law and the
traditions, neither he, nor his fellows, could
silence the mouths of these " ignorant and
unlearned men ", who were gaining converts
every day.

There were in the city of Jerusalem a
number of synagogues used by different sections
of the Jews. There was the Synagogue of the
Cyrenians and Alexandrians, of the Cilicians

and the Asians. As a Jew of Tarsus, Saul would attend that of the Cilicians. There he, no doubt, joined with those who carried on discussions with Stephen, the first martyr of the Christian Church. In these disputes Saul found all the knowledge he had gained at the feet of Gamaliel, and all that he had gained by his own studies, was useless ! Neither he nor his fellows were able to withstand the wisdom and the spirit by which Stephen spoke.

Imagine the effect such a failure must have had on the mind of Saul. He had spent years in studying the Law ; he knew all about the traditions of the fathers ; yet he could not silence this pestilent heretic !

As he and his fellows could not answer Stephen's arguments they brought him before the Sanhedrin. The charge against him was that he had spoken words against " this holy place " (the Temple), and the Law. There sat the members of the Council ; in front of them were a number of students, who were there to learn the ways of the Council. Among them, probably, was Saul. The whole procedure was a travesty of justice. No sentence was pronounced ; no adjournment to the next day as the Law provided in the case of a sentence of death. The councillors themselves rushed upon the prisoner, dragged him through the streets of the city, and then stoned him. The witnesses " laid down their garments at the feet of a young man named Saul ", who " was consenting " to Stephen's death. The word implies something more than this, as it is also rendered " be pleased ", and " have pleasure " ; it indicates that he was gratified by the action.

After the death of Stephen Saul threw himself heart and soul into the policy of persecuting the Nazarene heretics—he persecuted " the Way " unto the death.

Stephen's martyrdom had added something to the influences that were working within him, urging him, all unconsciously, towards the spirit that was to characterize him in the new life for which he was being prepared. He had been unable to answer the arguments adduced by Stephen. He had seen, or had been told of, Stephen's face " as it had been the face of an angel ", and he must have wondered why it should have had such an appearance. He had witnessed the stoning, heard the thud of the stones as they struck the body of the dying man, and he had heard the dying saint's last words, " Lord Jesus, receive my spirit ", and " Lord, lay not this sin to their charge ".

On a mind as sensitive as that of Saul such words must have made some impression. How could a follower of a so-called Messiah, who had been cursed in the manner of his death, look as Stephen had done ? How could he speak in the manner he had heard ? It was a problem for Saul—a problem he could not solve. All he could do was to put the problem away from him ; refuse to face it, and stifle all such thoughts by increasing his activity in the persecution that was taking place. He was a Jew! a rabbi! a teacher of the Law! He must not allow himself to be influenced by anything that came between him and his loyalty to the things for which he stood.

CHAPTER III

LIGHT FROM HEAVEN

To stifle the doubts that had arisen in his mind Saul plunged headlong into a policy of persecution. He would be loyal to the religion of his fathers, so he " laid waste the Church " ; ravaged it as a wild animal might uproot vines in a vineyard. Even that did not satisfy him, so he sought a wider field for his activities. He described his feelings towards the Christians at this time as " Being exceedingly mad against them, I persecuted them even unto strange cities ". He obtained an interview with the High Priest, told him of his desire, and asked for a commission to bring the Christians of Damascus to Jerusalem so that they might there receive punishment for their treachery to the religion in which they had been brought up. The High Priest at the time was Theophilus, a son of the Annas who had been concerned in the death of Jesus of Nazareth. Saul the Pharisee and Theophilus the Sadducee thus joined in the persecution of the followers of Jesus.

Armed with the desired authority, and accompanied by a band of men, Saul set his face northward, passed through the Damascus Gate of Jerusalem, and entered upon what proved to be one of the most momentous journeys ever undertaken. It was a journey of something like a hundred and fifty miles, and usually occupied some days. Saul was in no mood to lengthen the time any more than was necessary. Travel usually took place in the early and later hours of the day, with a siesta at noon. On this occasion there was no midday rest on the last day of the journey, for it was at that time that the incident occurred which changed the whole course of Saul's life.

Saul and his party had arrived within sight of Damascus. It was a beautiful sight; the houses looked like pearls in an emerald setting of vegetation; a great oasis in a desert of sand. But Saul had no eyes for the beauty; all he thought of was the work before him. Suddenly a vivid light from heaven, " above the brightness of the sun ", burst upon them, and Saul and all his party fell to the ground. From the midst of the light a voice spoke to Saul, spoke in the Hebrew tongue.

" Saul, Saul, why persecutest thou me? It is hard for thee to kick against the goad."

Terrible misgivings must have been caused by the question coming from the blinding light. Still, Saul answered the question.

" Who art thou, Lord? "

" I am Jesus whom thou persecutest."

How long had Saul been kicking against the goad, kicking like some fractious ox whose owner was urging him to follow in a required direction? Who can say? It may have dated from the time when he and others of Cilicia disputed in the synagogue with Stephen. It may have dated from the days when he heard the dying martyr's last words.

Now all questioning was over ; Saul could " kick " no longer ; he had heard, and he had seen, and the hearing and the seeing had convinced him that Jesus of Nazareth had been raised from the dead, and was alive. There was nothing more he could do. Somehow the curse which the Law placed upon those who were hanged had been removed. Everything now rested with Jesus and with God. So the conversation continued and Saul asked, " What shall I do, Lord ? "

" Rise and enter into the city ", was the answer, " and it shall be told thee what thou must do."

Men have argued about the appearance of Jesus to Saul. Did Saul really see Jesus ? The question is quite unnecessary. True the account does not say that Saul actually saw Jesus of Nazareth, but it certainly implies it. It says, for example, that the men who were with him heard the voice but saw no man, a remark which would be meaningless if Saul also heard the voice but saw no one. Later Ananias spoke to Saul and referred to Jesus who appeared to him in the way, and Barnabas used the same language when he took him to the apostles in Jerusalem. Years afterwards Saul wrote, " Last of all he was seen of me also ", and " Have not I seen Jesus our

Lord ? " With such explicit statements as these all questionings can be left.

When Saul arose he was blind ; the brilliance of the light, and the shock, had been too much for him, and he had to be led into Damascus by the men who had accompanied him. He entered into the city, not as an inquisitor commissioned by the High Priest, but as a humble follower of the crucified Nazarene. He had already acknowledged the change that had taken place in his status, for he had twice addressed him as " Lord ". The title implied much ; the one who had been the object of his persecution was recognized as Master and Lord. He was taken to a house in Straight Street, there to await the coming of one who would tell him what he was to do.

For three days he remained there sightless, and neither ate nor drank. During those three days the intimate knowledge he had gained of the Hebrew Scriptures came to his aid. In his enforced idleness he learned to see why One who met a felon's death outside the walls of Jerusalem should be the Messiah. One by one passages would come to his mind. There were allusions to Messiah the Prince who was to be cut off ; the Servant of the Lord who was to be given for a covenant of the people ; One who was to be despised and rejected of men, but who bore their sorrows and was wounded for their transgressions, and on whom God was to lay the iniquity of all. Saul was well acquainted with the Psalms, and there too he would recall many expressions that now took on a new meaning. In them were allusions to God's Holy One who was not to see corruption ; the Son of God's handmaid whose bonds were to be loosed.

Sayings like these, and many others, came to him, and as he thought of them he took refuge in that great source of consolation, and prayed for light and guidance. They were earnest prayers, for they came from the heart. Every reference to this period of his life shows how his past weighed on his spirit. As the light increased he was ready for the further instruction that had been promised.

On the third day of his darkness he heard the door of the house open, and footsteps approaching the door of the room where he lay. It was Ananias, a Christian of Damascus. Saul's fame as a persecutor had preceded him, and it had required two intimations to cause Ananias to pay him a visit. When he entered the chamber where Saul was, his first words were, " Brother Saul, the Lord, even Jesus, has sent me, that thou mayest receive thy sight, and be filled with the Holy Spirit ". What welcome words these must have been. " Brother Saul ! " addressed to him who had set out to take men like Ananias to Jerusalem to be punished.

Saul needed no convincing of the truth of the things that pertained to Jesus of Nazareth ; he knew he had been fighting against the truth ;

he had passed through the experience that is called conversion. There was only one thing more, and that was conveyed to him in the words of Ananias, " And now, why tarriest thou ? Arise and be baptized, and wash away thy sins ". Saul obeyed the injunction and was baptized. In that act, as he afterwards explained, he was buried with Christ in baptism into death. The old Saul was dead, and a new Saul, humbled and chastened, commenced a new life—a life in Christ.

The facts narrated above have a tremendous bearing on the truth of the gospel story. Saul was not an ordinary person. He was a clever and a well educated man, thoroughly grounded in the Jewish religion. He was in a position to talk to the men who had put Jesus to death. His new beliefs meant the ruin of the career for which all his former life had been a preparation ; it also meant a probable estrangement from his family. So far as this life was concerned, he had everything to lose, and nothing to gain, by becoming a follower of Jesus of Nazareth. Knowing all this, he submitted to the ordinance by which he was baptized into Christ—the crucified Nazarene ! Can it be imagined that anything short of absolute conviction that Jesus had been raised from the dead would have sufficed to cause him to give up everything he had hoped to be, and become a follower of Jesus ? He knew his new life must entail hardship, persecution, and probably death.

Before leaving Saul to face the new life upon which he had entered, one point may be noticed. Physically the effect of the blinding light that struck him to the ground seems never to have been overcome. At the end of the three days of darkness, when his sight was restored, there fell from his eyes " as it had been scales ", but his sight seems to have been permanently affected. Several incidents in his later life fit in with this suggestion ; perhaps the most direct evidence is the attitude of the Galatians, when he first preached the gospel to them ; they were willing, so he tells us, to have plucked out their own eyes and given them to him. Fortunately this disability in the matter of his physical eyesight did not cloud his mental vision, which has provided us with some of the most brilliant thoughts that are to be found in the New Testament ; they are second only to those of the Master himself.

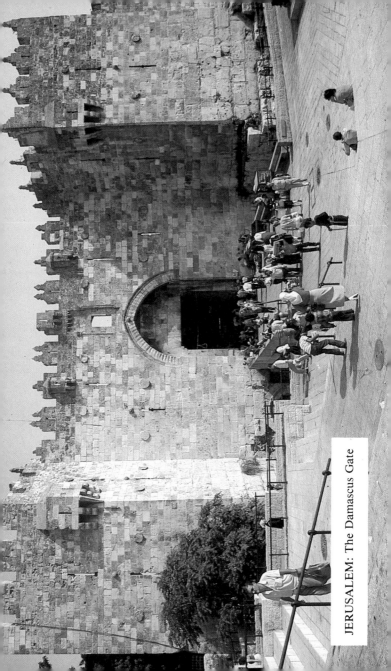

JERUSALEM: The Damascus Gate

VIA EGNATIA: View of the Roman road from Neapolis
to Philippi (modern Kavalla in the background)

CHAPTER IV

A CHANGED LIFE

THE change that took place in the life of Saul of Tarsus was fundamental ; old things had passed away, and all things had become new. Yet the new life was to be as strenuous as the old. His ardour was not damped, it was only turned into new channels. There was one way, however, in which the new life differed from that of his earlier days. The zeal was to be accompanied by constant suffering. That such would be the case he knew ; his own actions in the past would leave no doubt in his mind. Nevertheless, there was no hesitation, for it is written that he was certain days with the disciples that were at Damascus, and immediately he proclaimed Jesus that he is the Son of God.

The Jews of the city were astounded. They knew what he had been doing in Jerusalem, and why he had come to Damascus. Yet, here he was in the synagogues, teaching in a way that stultified everything for which he had formerly stood. As the days passed, and his knowledge increased, he confounded the Jews of Damascus, proving ever more powerfully that Jesus was the Messiah.

This phase of his life soon passed, for he went into Arabia. Arabia is a name of rather vague significance. Sometimes it was applied to the

district near Damascus, sometimes to the desert
that stretched from Syria to Egypt. Which part
Saul went to is not known. He went away
because it was still necessary for him to think
things out. He must think, not only of the truths
he had learned, but of how those truths affected
the old truths of Judaism. There was another
question he must face, and determine for himself.
What was he to do? What use was he to make
of his life?

These questions must be faced alone. His
whole future depended on the answers he gave
to them. The time was spent in seclusion, and
all the time his mind developed, and he gained
new insights into the meaning of the writings of
Moses and the Prophets. The time of quiet
would also help to tone down the shock of the
sudden revelation he had received, and prepare
him for the work he was to do. In later years
he laid it down as a principle that " a novice "
was not to be appointed to the work of publicly
proclaiming the truths of the gospel, and he
illustrated in himself the application of that
principle.

On his return to Damascus after this time of
quiet, he resumed his labours there, until the
Jews, unable to meet him in controversy, resorted
to the last way of a baffled cause, and formed a
conspiracy against his life. The gates of the city
were watched day and night, and assassins lay
in wait in various dark corners for an opportunity
to kill him. Eventually the Christians of

Damascus lowered him down from a house on the wall in a basket, and he made his way to Jerusalem. Three years before he had left that city as the accredited envoy of the High Priest to carry out his own design of putting an end to the heresy, as he deemed it, concerning the Messiahship of Jesus of Nazareth. Now he was returning as a fugitive, fleeing from his enemies (his former friends), because he preached that Jesus was the Christ. It seems likely that he avoided the more frequented roads and paths to the capital.

On his arrival he met with a bitter disappointment ; he was received there with suspicion ; the Christians of the city did not believe that the persecutor of the past was now a member of their body. They thought, probably, that he had professed conversion so that he might get information about them, and then betray them to the High Priest. It was natural for them to be suspicious. Three years was long enough for any rumours they might have heard of the change in his life to be forgotten, whereas the ferocity of the persecution with which he had been associated would be well remembered.

It was Barnabas, a Levite of Cyprus, who came to the rescue. Brought up in a Gentile land, his prejudices were less keen than those of the Christians of Jerusalem. He sought the disappointed Saul ; talked to him ; heard his account of what had occurred, and realized that he was a genuine Christian. Then he brought Saul to the apostles, and told them how the one-time persecutor had come to preach the truth he once destroyed.

If tradition may be relied upon, Barnabas had been at school at Tarsus, where he had met Saul. Now they had met again, and the meeting was to lead to great things.

Saul must have spent a wonderful fortnight in Jerusalem. He could talk with those who had seen and heard Jesus of Nazareth. He met Peter, the fisherman of Galilee. What tales he would have to tell of the things he had experienced when he accompanied Jesus in his wanderings! Of the things Jesus had done, and the things he had said. His parables; his encounters with the Pharisees (did Saul wince as he remembered that he had been one three years before?), his talks of his approaching death. Maybe Peter told of the way in which he had denied his Master, and of the utter desolation that overwhelmed him as Jesus had turned and looked at him. If so, he would have also told him how, in his despondency, he learned that Jesus had sent a special message to him— to him, the man who had sworn with oaths and curses that he had never known Jesus of Nazareth. He told him, too, of that unrecorded talk he had had with Jesus; how else would Saul have known of it, and written about it? Lastly, Peter would have told of those quiet talks by the Sea of Galilee, when Jesus had given him the threefold charge, " Feed My lambs ", " Tend My sheep ", " Feed My sheep ", to be set against his own threefold denial of his Master. Yes, they must have been wonderful days.

Then there were talks with James—James, the Lord's brother. He, too, would have much to tell. He had not believed in his brother while he was alive ; he and the family were not sure about him ; sometimes they thought he must be beside himself ! They had sincerely mourned his death ; his mother especially. Then Jesus had appeared to him ; to him, the disbelieving brother ! and he had become a devoted follower.

Perhaps Thomas was there, and Andrew and John, all of whom would have had something to say. These pleasant days soon passed ; they came to an end because Saul could not keep from talking about Jesus in Jerusalem, any more than he could in Damascus. He was too full of his knowledge of Jesus of Nazareth to keep quiet. Jesus was the Saviour of men ; who could keep such knowledge to himself ?

Taking all things into consideration, Saul could hardly have expected the Jews of Jerusalem to listen to him. They would look upon him as a renegade, a traitor to his past and to their religion. Yet he was bitterly disappointed. He thought he was specially qualified to speak to the Jews of Jerusalem about his new outlook on life. They must believe him ; they knew him ; they knew he had persecuted the Christians ; surely they would understand that nothing but the plainest demonstration of the fact that Jesus of Nazareth had been raised from the dead would have caused him to make such a tremendous change.

Perhaps nothing illustrates the courage of Saul better than this desire to preach Christ in Jerusalem. Those with whom he would have talked were the very class with whom he had been associated in the past, and it would have required a large amount of moral courage for him to face them and say that all he had contended for in the past was wrong. It would have been much easier to carry on such a work in other places. Did something within him urge him on to take the place that had formerly been occupied by Stephen?

Saul was depressed at the way in which his efforts were received. In the circumstances he took the best course open to him; he went into the Temple, and poured out his troubles to God. There he fell into a trance, and again heard the voice of Jesus speaking to him. The voice said, " Make haste, and get thee quickly out of Jerusalem, because they will not receive of thee testimony concerning Me ".

Saul could not understand it. Honest and straightforward himself, he could not understand why others should not believe him as he recounted his experiences. Jesus knew better, and when Saul urged his ideas, he answered, " Depart, for I will send thee forth far hence unto the Gentiles ".

The Christians of Jerusalem urged the same thing upon him. He could do nothing in

Jerusalem or in Damascus ; his life was in danger in either city. They did what they could for him ; they " brought him down to Caesarea ", forming a peaceful body-guard about him until he found safety in a ship going to Tarsus. One rather wonders whether they breathed a sigh of relief when they saw the ship sail. Men of Saul's temperament can be a danger.

After Saul left Jerusalem it is said in the Acts that " so the Church throughout all Judea, and Galilee, and Samaria, had peace, being edified ; and, walking in the fear of the Lord and in the comfort of the Holy Spirit, was multiplied ". It was not Saul's departure that caused this change ; it was due to an alteration in the political situation. Caligula, the Emperor of the Roman world, was a friend of Herod Agrippa, and the Jews anticipated great things from his accession. Their hopes were disappointed. Caligula arrogated to himself divine honours, and gave orders that a statue of himself should be placed in the Temple at Jerusalem. Nothing could have exasperated the Jews more than this. Indignation and resentment flamed forth. Everything else was forgotten, and this insane attempt by a Roman Emperor brought freedom from persecution to the Christians. The Church had peace.

CHAPTER V

A CALL TO SERVICE

THE great hopes which had caused Saul to go to Jerusalem had led to nothing. His flight to Tarsus, for that is how it must have appeared to him, was a tame ending to the adventure. His attempt to preach Christ in the Holy City had failed ; he had accomplished nothing ; even his meetings with the Apostles and other Christians, however interesting they may have been, seem to have had little effect. They had shown brotherly solicitude for his safety, but it is probable that even among the believers of the Capital there were still those who were sceptical about him and his work.

What were Saul's thoughts as he sailed over the waters of the Mediterranean towards Tarsus ? If his father and mother were still alive he must have wondered how they would meet him now that he was a follower of Jesus of Nazareth. His father had taken a pride in him as a disciple of the great Gamaliel, and as a rabbi among the people. That seemed a long way back now, so much had happened. He certainly would not have changed his position ; he knew him on whom he believed, and that One had said, as perhaps Peter had told him, " Lo, I am with you alway ". Strong in that belief he trod once again the familiar streets of

Tarsus, which was to be his home for a long time.

What did he do during the years he remained there ; years in which he reached his fortieth birthday ? What were his relations with his parents, if they were alive ? What did his sister think of him ? We can only surmise, for nothing is recorded concerning the whole time he remained in his native city. There are grounds for thinking that he was disowned by his father ; disowned with bitter words. The fervent Pharisee had no use for a son who had chosen to become a follower of the Nazarene, a member of the " sect " everywhere spoken against.

It may have been the memory of some such incident that caused him to write in after years, " Fathers, provoke not your children that they be not discouraged ". " Ye fathers, provoke not your children." If his father did disown him he would have to earn his living at his trade of cloth-weaving and tent-making. He would sit at it, working and thinking. Probably his thoughts would not have been of the pleasantest kind. What had he accomplished at the age of forty ? Outwardly it looked as if the only result was the estrangement of his family, after they had made such sacrifices for him. That and his flight from Damascus, and his flight, for such it must have seemed to be, from Jerusalem.

It may be taken for granted, however, that he did not keep silent on the great truth he had received. From all we know of Saul of Tarsus that would have been impossible, but of the incidents of his stay in his own city we know nothing.

To pick up the thread of the story it is necessary to go to Antioch. At that time Antioch was the third city of the world, the Queen of the East ; a Greek city enriched by the Romans and by Herod the Great, who had gone out of his way to add to its magnificence. He had built a street through the city, four miles long, with a colonnade of white marble. The population of the city was about half a million, made up of various nationalities. It was a frivolous, pleasure-loving city, morally corrupt. A poet has said of it,

> Long since the stream that wanton Syria laves,
> Has disembogued its filth in Tiber's waves,
> Its language, its arts, o'erwhelmed us with the scum
> Of Antioch's streets, its minstrels, harp and drum.

It was written of Antioch : " It seems as though it were a law of human intercourse that when races are commingled in large masses, the worst qualities of each appear intensified in the general iniquity ". It is strange indeed that such a city should have been the place that introduced Saul to renewed activity, and opened to him his life's work.

The bitterness of the persecution that had followed the death of Stephen caused many of the disciples to be scattered, and as they went to various parts they preached the word, but only to Jews. There were, however, some who came from Cyprus and Cyrene to Antioch, and these preached to Greeks also. Their efforts met with an immediate response, and a considerable number believed. News of this unexpected development reached the Church at Jerusalem, where it raised a difficult problem, and it was decided to send Barnabas to see what was happening. When Barnabas arrived at Antioch he recognized the great possibilities that were being opened up. Increasing numbers meant increasing work. He thought of Saul, who seemed to be just the man for such a work, and at once journeyed to Tarsus to seek him.

For the second time Saul owed an introduction to Barnabas. He was evidently quite willing to leave Tarsus and seek a wider field for his activities. He threw himself into the work, and was at last in a congenial atmosphere. It was the beginning of his real life's work.

For twelve months the work at Antioch continued to engross him. It must have been a happy time for Saul; he was meeting with a Church marked by a great activity; he was with Barnabas, and he began to be known to, and appreciated by, the believers in the city.

Two incidents that occurred in the Church at Antioch call for attention. During the time

Saul was there certain prophets came from Jerusalem, one of whom, named Agabus, speaking by inspiration, foretold that a dearth would afflict " all the world ", an expression which in this case, as in several others, means primarily the Roman Empire. Such a phenomenon would cause special suffering to the Christians of Jerusalem. They were, generally speaking, composed of the poor of the world, and they would certainly be disregarded by the priests in any arrangements that might be made for the relief of the sufferers in Jerusalem. In these circumstances the disciples in Antioch determined to send relief to the brethren in Judea. This is the first mention of a practice which has ever since been a characteristic of Christianity ; no other system of religion can claim anything like the same amount of that particular virtue.

The contributions of the Church at Antioch were sent to Jerusalem by Barnabas and Saul. The selection was a happy one. Barnabas had been sent to Antioch by the Church at Jerusalem, of which he had been a member from the earliest days, and it gave the members of the Church there an opportunity to become better acquainted with Saul.

It has been seen that the Church at Antioch was largely composed of Gentiles, and this contribution was the first illustration of a principle that Saul spoke of in later years, " If the Gentiles have been made partakers of their (the Jews') spiritual things, they owe it to them also to minister unto them in carnal things ". In acting on this principle it was desirable that there should be at least one representative of the Gentile element of the Antiochian Church in the party that carried the bounty to Jerusalem, and Titus was chosen for this purpose.

There seems to have been some discussion about the advisability of circumcising Titus before he accompanied Saul and Barnabas on this errand of mercy. On this point Saul was adamant. Titus was going as one of the party ; he and they were carrying alms to the Church, and Saul positively refused to give way to certain people whom he described as "false brethren privily brought in ". They were evidently a Pharisaic group among the Christians of Jerusalem, and the trouble they caused was a precurser of a greater one in the future.

They arrived in the city at a time of tribulation. James, the brother of John, had been slain by Herod Agrippa, and Peter had been put in prison, from whence he had been miraculously delivered. Persecution however, failed to accomplish the purpose for which it had been instituted, for the " Word of the Lord grew and multiplied ".

Saul and Barnabas evidently stayed in Jerusalem for some time. The relief was provided in kind, and they had been appointed to act as the administrators. The word used in the Greek for their service is *diakonian*, from the term used to designate the seven " deacons " who had been appointed to carry on a somewhat similar work in Jerusalem in the earliest days of the Church. They probably stayed during the time covered by the famine, and when they returned to Antioch, they took with them John, whose surname was Mark.

The work in Antioch still prospered, and a feeling seems to have grown up that something more should be done. At a meeting of the Church that " something more " was indicated. There were present on one occasion Barnabas, Symeon Niger (Niger means black), Lucius of Cyrene, and Manaen, the foster-brother of Herod, and Saul. All these are described as prophets and teachers. The mention of Manaen indicates that whilst " not many wise after the flesh, not many mighty, not many noble are called ", yet, both then, and since, some few such have been called to follow the Master. It is rather a pleasing speculation that Manaen may have received his call through Joanna, the wife of Chusa, Herod's steward.

As the brethren who have been named ministered to the Lord, and fasted, the Spirit said, " Separate to me Barnabas and Saul, for the work to which I have called them ". The time of wonderment about the next development was over. A time of fasting and prayer ensued, then they laid their hands upon Barnabas and Saul, and sent them forth on their mission.

The incident is simply told in a very few words, and no one reading it for the first time would imagine that one of the greatest tasks ever set before men was being inaugurated. Try to imagine that task. Two men, Barnabas and Saul, had been called to undertake it. Before them was a world steeped in paganism, with all its associations of moral depravity. Their object was to proclaim to peoples wholly given up to the ways of unenlightened flesh the gospel of the Kingdom of God, a kingdom which, under the rule of a Messiah who had been rejected by his own people and crucified by the Romans, would eventually subvert every kingdom and institution, and in so doing bring about a time when all the nations of the earth would be blessed. Their message was not from any earthly potentate, nor was it from any influential party or people. They carried no insignia of office ; no herald announced their departure or their arrival. Their only send-off had been fasting and prayer, but their credentials were to be the " demonstration of the Spirit and power ".

Ordinary individuals might have been appalled as they faced such a task. There was nothing to indicate that they were exceptional people ; so far as Saul was concerned, people said of him that his bodily presence was weak and his speech was of no account. An early tradition tells how one who was sent out to meet him was told to look for a man of moderate stature, with scanty curly hair, crooked legs, blue eyes, large knit eyebrows, and a long nose. There was obviously nothing imposing in such a man, but whatever his appearance may have been his body was as tempered steel. From the beginning he proved to be the main-spring of the enterprise.

As a kind of footnote, after speaking of their setting out, it is said that they had John Mark as their attendant. He was a relative of Barnabas, and apparently, had not been appointed by the Church.

The three men left Antioch for its port, Seleucia, whence they took ship to Cyprus. This was probably due to the fact that Barnabas was a native of that island, and had a desire to make known to its people the great truths he had learned. Sailing over the Great Sea, they landed at Salamis on the east coast of the island, where the Jews were fairly numerous. The record speaks of the synagogues there ; the term in the plural is not used in connection with any other place that was visited. Nothing is recorded of their work except that they preached the word of God in the synagogues, though Barnabas probably met old friends who would welcome him and his fellow travellers.

As they passed through the island they preached at various places until they reached Paphos, the residence of the Roman Proconsul, Sergius Paulus, who is described as a man of understanding. News of their journey had reached him, and he had doubtless heard something of the character of the message they were delivering. He sent for them, and in response

Barnabas and Saul attended on him and preached the word of the Lord. It was the first time the messengers of Christ had proclaimed his word to a Roman governor.

They were withstood by a certain Jew, Elymas, or Bar-Jesus, who is described as a sorcerer and a false prophet. The age was one in which magical rites were widely practised ; in those days there was no well defined line between astronomy and astrology, or between medicine and magic. When Elymas saw that Sergius Paulus was listening intently to the words of Saul, he saw that if the proconsul received them his influence over the governor would be ended. He noticed, as one manuscript puts it, that the proconsul was " listening with much pleasure to them ". If that went on it meant the end of all his gains, and that, he decided, must not happen. So he began to contradict Saul, and did all he could to divert the proconsul's attention. His oppostition called forth the indignation of Saul. He " fastened his eyes " upon him, saying, " O full of all guile and all craft, thou son of the devil, thou enemy of all righteousness, wilt thou not cease to pervert the right ways of the Lord ? And now, lo, the hand of the Lord is upon thee, and thou shalt be blind, not seeing the sun for a season."

At once a mist and darkness fell upon him, and he felt around for some one to take him by the hand. It was a sign to the governor ; he believed, and Sergius Paulus was the first

41

prominent Roman to adopt the faith of Christ.

Nothing more is said of the work in Cyprus, and it is not known how long they stayed, nor what results followed.

One significant thing stands out in the record of the incident. Hitherto every allusion to the two men has spoken of Barnabas and Saul ; now it is Paul and Barnabas, or Paul and his company. The work in Cyprus showed the unquestioned leadership of Saul ; his Hebrew name now disappears, and the more familiar name of Paul is introduced. They were now facing the Roman world, and Saul adopted his Roman name—Paul.

CHAPTER VI

THE GOSPEL IN ASIA MINOR

PAUL and his company secured a passage in a vessel sailing for Asia Minor in which they journeyed to Perga, a town on the River Cestrus, about seven miles from the coast. Nothing is said of any work being done there, and the record is tantalisingly brief. At this point they lost the company of John Mark, who left them, and " went not with them to the work ". It was an unpromising beginning for them, and an equally unpromising beginning of the career of Mark. No reason is given for his failure to go further. He may have been anxious about the welfare of his mother in Jerusalem, or he may have shirked the dangers that were to be anticipated from the journey Paul and Barnabas had undertaken, which would lead them into the interior of the country. His desertion, for so it appeared to be to Paul, was evidently a serious disappointment, though in later days he was able to speak of Mark as " profitable for the ministry ".

The country before them was a difficult one ; inscriptions have been found which refer to the " perils " of the district ; perils of rivers and perils of robbers, two of the items mentioned in the Foreword.

Something evidently happened at Perga which caused a change in the arrangements of

Paul and Barnabas. The district round Perga is warm and enervating. In the evening mists arise, and the heat of the day is succeeded by a feeling of chilliness. The marshes around breed mosquitoes, and they in turn cause malaria. Paul seems to have been affected by the latter and became a very sick man. That was why he felt Mark's departure so severely. Though the Acts says nothing of this, the Epistle to the Galatians does. Antioch in Pisidia, to which the two missionaries went, was in Galatia, and in the Epistle Paul wrote to the Christians of that province he says that he first preached to them " because of an infirmity of the flesh ", which he also describes as " a temptation to you in my flesh "—a temptation, not to him, but to them. Yet they neither despised nor rejected him. The language used suggests an illness that affected him in such a way that they might have been tempted to despise him for it. It seems to have been a kind of malaria which, from time to time, caused prostration and other symptoms.

As the victim of an illness of this kind there was only one thing to be done, and that was to get away from Perga as soon as possible, leaving the low and enervating climate for the cooler air of the highlands to the north, and that is what they did.

Leaving the coastal district, Paul and Barnabas started on their journey which must have taken them several days. As they reached the higher ground Paul would gain strength, and by the time they arrived at Antioch he was probably well on the way to recovery. On this journey, however, he may have experienced the perils referred to. The rivers of the district are subject to sudden and violent changes, dashing suddenly down through narrow ravines, sweeping away anything that might have been caught by them. In the rocky caverns by the roadside robbers lurked to surprise unwary travellers. Further on it was safer, as the Romans had caused a road to be built to permit the rapid transit of soldiers whose duty it was to put down this particular kind of peril.

The journey led them through grand and beautiful scenery. Paul never refers to anything of that kind ; probably he was too much a man of the city to admire the beauty of natural things. Unlike his Master he does not seem to have been impressed by the beauty of nature, the flowers of the field, or the birds of the air ; his illustrations are taken rather from scenes in cities, foundations and buildings, the incidents of the arena, and the arms and accoutrements of the soldier.

In a few days Paul and Barnabas reached Antioch, a city of the same name as the one from which they had set out. Antioch in Pisidia was a place of importance, a Roman colony, and a military depot. It was not, however, to the ordinary population of the city that they addressed themselves. True to the principles that guided him, Paul spoke first to the Jews.

There was a synagogue in Antioch, and on the first Sabbath of their stay the two entered it, and sat down. After the prayers, and the readings from the Law and the Prophets, they were invited to address the assembly, which was composed of Jews (" Men of Israel ") and proselytes (" ye that fear God "). It was Paul, not the more impressive looking Barnabas, who responded. He stood up, beckoned with his hand (a characteristic gesture of his) and commenced to speak. As it is his first recorded address it is worthy of some consideration. It was very different from most of the discourses that are given at the present time, for it was a long and sustained argument based upon the history of Israel, with constant quotations from, and allusions to, the Old Testament.

Expressions such as those that follow illustrate the method he adopted. " According to promise ", " The promise made unto the fathers ", " As also it is written ", " He hath spoken on this wise ", " He saith also in another place ", " That which is spoken in the prophets". In the course of twenty-five verses there were several direct references to scriptural statements, to say nothing of the fact that the whole of the first portion of the address was an outline of Israel's history as given in the Scriptures.

It will be interesting to notice a peculiarity of these historical allusions. " The God of this people Israel chose our fathers, and exalted the people when they sojourned in the land of Egypt,

and with a high arm led he them forth out of it."
He "destroyed seven nations in the land of
Canaan". He "gave them their land for an
inheritance". "He gave them judges." "God
gave unto them Saul the son of Kish." "When
he had removed him, he raised up David to be
their king." This is a method of treating
history which is not found in modern histories.
Most historians see nothing in history but the
clashing of various forces, working out an end
which cannot be foreseen. Paul saw God in the
history of Israel, and his words are both interesting and suggestive.

There was an inner theme to his discourse.
Up to this point that portion of his audience
referred to as "Men of Israel" had no doubt
listened with interest and satisfaction, but he
had no intention of continuing in this way ; he
had an object in view. He had led them to think
of David, a name always attractive to Jewish
ears. Striking a chord familiar to his hearers,
he said, "Of this man's seed hath God, according
to promise brought unto Israel a Saviour,
Jesus".

Having reached this point, he lightly
sketched the mission of John the Baptist, and
then fixed the attention of his hearers on Jesus of
Nazareth. He showed how the Jews of Jerusalem had fulfilled the predictions of the prophets
by condemning him, insisting that he should be
put to death when Pilate did what he could to
save him. Then followed the crux of the address,

the startling statement that God had raised Jesus from the dead !

It was a strange message to people who had never heard it before ; strange enough to call for something more than the bare assertion that it had taken place. Paul therefore went on to tell them that there were witnesses who could testify to the truth of what had he spoken. " He was seen for many days of them that came up with him from Galilee to Jerusalem, who are now his witnesses unto the people."

These witnesses, however, were hundreds of miles away, and the Jews and proselytes of Antioch of Pisidia could hardly be expected to accept their testimony on the statement of an itinerant preacher of whom they knew nothing. Paul therefore passed to other evidence ; he appealed to their own Scriptures. Had not God said in the book of Psalms, " Thou art my Son, this day have I begotten thee "? That might not sound a very convincing proof of the resurrection of Jesus, but there was no getting away from another statement in the Psalms, " Thou wilt not give thy Holy One to see corruption ". That could not refer to David, for he did see corruption, as Paul went on to show, " David, after he had in his own generation served the counsel of God, fell on sleep, and was laid unto his fathers, and saw corruption ; but he whom God raised up saw no corruption ".

In the circumstances there was no gainsaying that the Psalm applied to someone other than David. The hearers might question the speaker's assertion about the resurrection of Jesus of Nazareth, they might ignore the testimony of men whom they could not examine ; but there was no getting away from the statements of their own Scriptures. They were too scrupulously careful of them to question their authority, so the speaker had proved his case. There was something more, however. Left just here the address would have been interesting, provocative perhaps, but it would have led nowhere—hence the words that followed. " Be it known unto you, brethren, that through this man is proclaimed unto you remission of sins ; and by him every one that believeth is justified from all things from which ye could not be justified by the Law of Moses."

At this point restlessness set in among many of the listeners. There were signs of anger among them. What would this strange preacher say next ? He had reviled the leaders of their people, charging them with responsibility for the death of the Son of David ! Paul stayed for a moment or two, looking around at his restless audience, then he spoke again. " Behold, ye despisers, and wonder, and perish, for I work a work in your days, a work which ye shall in no wise believe if one declare it unto you." It was another thrust from their own Scriptures.

The meeting broke up ; many had been interested, and asked that more might be said on the next Sabbath. Some went further ; they followed Paul and Barnabas, who spoke to them, adding to the information that had already been given, and urging them to continue in God's grace.

Among the Jews and proselytes of Antioch there was one great topic of conversation during the week ; the strange things that had been spoken in the synagogue on the Sabbath. The Jewish leaders were annoyed. They had never aroused such an interest in the city, and they bitterly resented the success of the strange preacher. It was different with the proselytes ; they also talked ; talked among themselves, and to the people whom they met. The result was that on the following Sabbath almost the whole city crowded around to hear what the strange speaker had to say. That was too much for the Jews. Such a thing had never before been seen in the city. In the Jewish Scriptures there was a saying, " Jealousy is as cruel as the grave " ; and the Jews of Antioch gave an illustration of it. As soon as Paul began to speak he was interrupted. Shouts came from various parts of the synagogue ; Jews contradicted the speaker ; they went so far as to blaspheme and rail on him as only angry men can rail.

It was a turning point in the work at Antioch, and Paul and Barnabas spoke out plainly. The Jews had thrust the Word of God from them, so Paul announced that they would turn to the Gentiles. In taking this course he established his position from the Jewish Scriptures, in which it is written, " I have set thee for a light of the

Gentiles, that thou shouldest be for salvation unto the uttermost part of the earth ". What the Jews rejected the Gentiles rejoiced in ; for when they heard Paul's saying " they were glad and glorified the word of God ", and many of them believed it. They showed their feelings in a practical way. Paul was still a sick man, still suffering from the trouble that had overtaken him at Perga, yet, as he reminded them afterwards in a letter, they " received him as an angel of God ".

The events in Antioch may be regarded as the real commencement of Paul's work. His preaching was not confined to the city of Antioch, for the word spread through the various districts in the region controlled from that city.

The enmity of the Jews remained. The success of the work only made them the more embittered. As Antioch was a Roman colony they could not invoke the law, so they adopted other means. Working through the chief men of the city, some of whom were probably related to the women proselytes to Judaism, they stirred up a persecution against Paul and Barnabas, and finally succeeded in expelling them beyond their borders. Various acts of persecution preceded the expulsion ; Paul mentions them in his letter to Timothy : " Thou didst follow my teaching, conduct, purpose, faith, longsuffering, love, patience, persecutions, sufferings, what things befell me at Antioch ... what persecutions I endured ". The language suggests a long drawn out persecution, not a sudden blaze up at the last minute.

In accordance with the instructions the Master had given to his messengers in Palestine, when Paul and Barnabas were driven from the city, they took off their sandals, and shook the dust from them. They were then once more on the road, but their labour had not been in vain. " As many as were ordained to eternal life believed " " throughout all the region ".

The first of the Churches of Galatia had been established, and that was no small accomplishment.

CHAPTER VII

THE END OF THE FIRST JOURNEY

WHEN they were expelled from Antioch Paul and
Barnabas made their way along the road known
as the Via Regalis to Iconium, some sixty, or
more, miles to the south-east. Still acting on the
principle of " to the Jew first ", they visited the
synagogue where they so spoke that a great
multitude of Jews and Greeks believed. It
looked as if a successful work might be carried
on here. They were not given much time to
rejoice in such an anticipation. The envy that
had caused the cessation of the work in Antioch
soon grew up in Iconium. The malice of those
of the Jews who would not receive their teaching
found a means to raise the feelings against those
who received the Apostle's doctrine. Wherever
Paul went the preaching of the Cross was a
stumbling-block to the Jews ; they were ready
enough to listen to him when he spoke of the past
of their nation, or when he referred to the
prophecies that spoke of the coming of a Messiah
and Redeemer, but when he went on to show
how that Messiah had suffered death by crucifixion, they shut their ears, even though the
message included the news that he had been
raised from the dead.

The prejudice of the Jews did not cause Paul
to cease his labours. The work was too im-

portant, and because of the prejudice, and the incipient persecution that manifested itself, Paul and Barnabas continued for a long time to preach Jesus and the Kingdom. The impression made by their words was deepened by the fact that these were confirmed by the signs and wonders they were enabled to do.

Such works did not stop the animosity of the Jews, and in the end the city was divided over the matter, one part siding with the Jews and the other with the Apostles. The unruly section of the populace, made up of Jews and Greeks, encouraged by the rulers of the city, proceeded to violence, and Paul and Barnabas were in danger of being stoned. They became aware of what was intended, and left the city, going on to Lystra, which is described as a city of Lycaonia. Here they were in circumstances that differed from any they had experienced before. They were in a Roman colony, but its population seems to have been small, and was largely composed of a ruder native race. There is no mention of a synagogue, so the Jews in Lystra must have been few.

Here they carried on their work of proclaiming the gospel. On one occasion when they were so engaged an event happened that led to a new feature in Paul's experiences. Hitherto the opposition he had met, and the persecutions he had endured, were the result of Jewish animosity ; he had suffered, to use his words, from " perils by his own countrymen " ; now he was to experience the next clause, " perils by the heathen ".

Among those who were listening to the proclamation was a cripple. The author of the Acts, Luke, who was a physician, is very definite in describing the man, for he says of him that he was impotent in his feet, that he had been lame from his birth, and had never walked. He was listening intently to what Paul was saying, and Paul realized that he had faith to be healed. He " fastened his eyes " on the man, and said, " Stand upright upon thy feet ". The cripple not only stood, he leaped, as if to demonstrate the completeness of the cure.

The effect on the people was remarkable. They were simple folk, and reasoned that such a work could not have been done by mere men, so that some of their gods had come to their city, and were thus giving witness to their presence. The wording of the record shows that they were deeply stirred. In this outlying province of the Roman Empire the Greek language would be understood, and spoken. But the wonder they had witnessed broke down the barrier of language ; Greek was an acquired tongue, and in moments of excitement native language and native ways assert themselves. It was so now, and they exclaimed in their own language, " The gods are come down to us in the likeness of men !"

Lystra was addicted to the worship of Zeus, the greatest of the Greek gods, to whom a temple was dedicated. The temple was situated just outside the gate of the city. The people decided that one of the visiting deities must be Zeus, and they gave that name to Barnabas, because he was the more imposing of the two. They named Paul Hermes, a god associated with inventions and versatility, the god of eloquence, and, for that reason, the messenger of the gods, They gave it to Paul because he was the chief speaker !

In passing, it is worth noting that in the letter to the churches of Galatia (one of which was the Church at Lystra), Paul speaks of the believers there having received him as a messenger of God. Our Bible says " angel ", but the Greek is *angellon*.

The words of the people, having been spoken in their native tongue, were not understood by Paul or Barnabas, who went their way, probably desiring to get away from the excited crowd. Soon afterwards there was a commotion in the city. News of what had happened spread, and soon reached the priest of the temple of Zeus outside the gates, who presently approached the house in which Paul and Barnabas were staying, bringing oxen which he intended to sacrifice to the illustrious visitors.

As soon as Paul and Barnabas realized what was happening they acted. Had they been self-seekers this was their opportunity. Acclaimed as gods by the whole population of the city, they might have accepted the homage, and traded upon it. Instead they rushed among the people, rending their clothes, and beseeching them to desist from their purpose.

They further spoke to them, and as the record of what they said is the first we have of an address given to a purely Gentile audience it is worthy of consideration. Here it is.

> "Men, why do ye these things? We also are men of like passions with you, and bring you good tidings that ye should turn from these vain things unto the living God, who made heaven, and the earth and the sea, and all that in them is; who in the generations gone by suffered all nations to walk in their own ways. And yet he left not himself without witness, in that he did good and gave you from heaven rains and fruitful seasons, filling your hearts with food and gladness."

Of course the foregoing is only a summary of what was said, yet it illustrates Paul's methods. The words were quite different from what he would have put before a Jewish audience, or to an audience that included a number of proselytes. He spoke of fundamental matters which cut at the root of the religious ideas of his hearers. There was no room for Zeus and Hermes, or any other of their supposed gods. One God, by whatever name He might be known, had made the heavens and the earth, and all the good things which the earth produced for the use of man. It was an attempt to fix the minds of his hearers on the One God—the living and the true God, which he afterwards preached to the people of Thessalonica.

The point of human responsibility which he introduced, and the statement that He suffered all nations to walk in their own ways in the past, will come up for notice later in the account of an address given at Athens.

The result of this address at Lystra was that the sacrifice did not take place, but the disavowal of divinity left the people puzzled. No doubt there were questions and talks. One can imagine the reasoning of the people. If these men are not gods, how were they able to cure the cripple? Was it by magic? Was it by demonic agency? So the ground was prepared for the incidents that followed.

Jewish spite followed them. From Iconium and from Antioch, Jews came to Lystra. There they heard of the doings of Paul since he left their neighbourhoods, and they worked upon the feelings of the people. It was easy to do this now; repudiating divinity, Paul and Barnabas had laid themselves open to Jewish suggestions, and the streets of Lystra rang with shouts of "Stone him". Soon the stones began to fly. It was not a regular stoning judicially ordered as that of Stephen had been; it was a case of mob law. As the stones struck him in various parts of his body, did Paul's thoughts go back to the day, which must have seemed so long ago, when the witnesses against Stephen had laid their clothes at the feet of a young man named Saul?

The stoning was soon over; as one struck him, Paul fell to the ground. The mob, or some of its members, then dragged him through the streets, past the temple where sacrifices were to have been offered in his honour, and left him for dead, outside the city.

Saul was not dead. His work was beginning, not finished. As a number of disciples stood round the bruised body, he moved, probably a tremor passed through him; then he slowly arose, and, surrounded and supported by sympathetic disciples, made his way back into the city.

Among those who had stood there sorrowfully regarding what they thought was the dead body of their revered teacher, was a youth, accompanied, maybe, by his mother and, possibly, his grandmother. Their names were Timothy, Lois, and Eunice, the Timothy who became one of the best beloved of all Paul's followers, his dearest friend. Timothy was a native of Lystra. He was a disciple when Paul visited the town on his second journey, and Paul speaks of him as his beloved child; his true child in the faith. He must therefore have been converted by the Apostle, and it must have taken place during this, his first, visit. Timothy must have been young at the time, for almost twenty years afterwards, Paul wrote, " Let no man despise thy youth ". Fortunately he had received good training before the time of his conversion. His mother and grandmother had been women of unfeigned faith, and it is said of him that from a babe he had known the Sacred Writings—the Holy Scriptures.

The stoning, though not fatal, brought an end to Paul's labours in Lystra ; whatever might be possible on a later occasion nothing more could be done now. Twenty miles away there was another city, Derbe, and thither Paul and Barnabas, the former bruised and suffering, made their way. Nothing is known of the reception they had there, all that is said is that they preached the gospel, and made many disciples. They stayed there for some time, during which Paul carried on his trade, telling all who would stop to listen the story of Jesus of Nazareth, and his promised return.

The subsequent course of Paul and Barnabas is instructive. Amid discouragement and persecution they had proclaimed Christ crucified in various places. Three times they had been compelled to flee. Now at Derbe, they were within a hundred miles of Tarsus, though it was not always possible to travel there as floods made a portion of the road impassable. But the proximity of Tarsus, and the troubles they had experienced on their journeys, did not prevent them retracing their steps and returning by the way they had come. In doing so they risked the danger of stirring up the same animosity as had assailed them before, though they were helped, to some extent, by the fact that, in the meantime, new Roman magistrates had been appointed in the various cities.

Their object in retracing their steps was not so much to preach the gospel, as to attend to matters of equal importance in organizing the companies of believers, and to exhort and upbuild their converts. Among other things they told them it was through many tribulations that they must enter the Kingdom of God. Serving Christ is not an easy matter.

In carrying out this purpose they formed the believers in each place into a church, in which elders were appointed to carry out the various duties that were essential to the welfare of its members. This was done at impressive meetings at which they prayed and fasted before the appointed elders were commended to the Lord. There was nothing haphazard in Paul's work for Christ.

Having left things in order, Paul and Barnabas definitely turned their faces to Antioch in Syria, the city from which they had started out. On the way they preached in Perga, where, it will be remembered they had not spoken on their outward journey. The fact shows that it was no ordinary cause that kept them from doing so when they passed through the city before ; there must have been some special reason for passing through it so quickly, and that must have been the illness which has been mentioned.

They had done a great work, and some might have felt that others should carry it on while they stayed in the congenial surroundings of Antioch and the churches in Syria. Neither Paul, nor Barnabas, was a man of that type. They knew the Truth ; they knew men were perishing for want of that Truth, so they must preach it whatever the consequences might be. Yet they needed a rest after the labours and sufferings they had endured, so, after they had given the Church in Antioch an account of their experiences, and told how God had opened the door of faith to the Gentiles, they tarried there " no little time ".

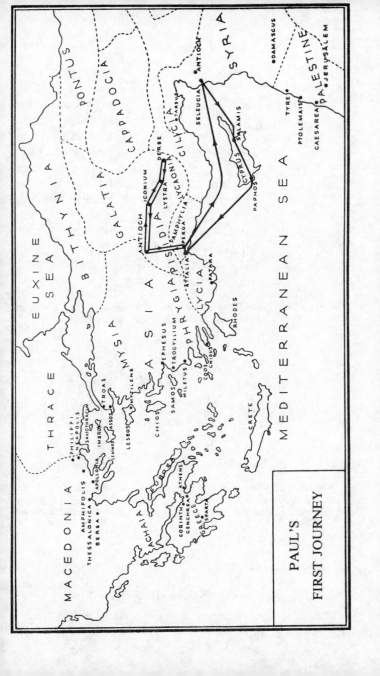

PAUL'S
FIRST JOURNEY

Coin of Herod Agrippa II
(but note that the head is that of the Emperor Titus)

A brass coin from Ephesus on which the name of the "townclerk"
of the time is inscribed (cf. Acts 19:35)

Reverse of silver medallion
of Claudius and Agrippina,
showing figure and name of
Diana of the Ephesians

Coin of the district of Lydia
in Asia Minor—"They do it
to obtain a corruptible crown"
(1 Cor. 9:25; 2 Tim. 2:5)

COINS OF PAUL'S DAY

CHAPTER VIII

A CRISIS IN THE CHURCH

THE period that immediately followed Paul's return from his first great journey was, probably, one of the happiest of his career. He had carried out a Divine charge, and though it had been associated with persecutions and a stoning, he was still alive, and was surrounded by a number of kindred spirits with whom he would rejoice in the work that had been done, and in the prospect of further opportunities. There was much to do, and Paul was never willingly an idle man. He would take active part in the work at Antioch ; preaching, exhorting, organizing, making tentative plans for future activities ; all this would fill up his time in an agreeable way. He was happy, the work was prospering, yet there were signs of a coming change. There were discussions, disputations.

By this time people of various classes had been gathered into the gospel net. At first the fervour of conversion kept them happy and united, though the discerning eye saw grave possibilities for the future. Among those who had recognized the Messiahship of Jesus of Nazareth were priests and Pharisees. Some of these did not appreciate the liberty wherewith Christ had made them free. It is not to be wondered at that it should have been so. Jewish exclusiveness was a very strong characteristic of these people ; it had taken a thrice repeated vision, and a definite command, to cause Peter to go to the house of Cornelius. As the number of Gentile believers increased the old feeling asserted itself in some of the Jews, and a party arose in the Church which contended that Gentile believers should submit to the rite of circumcision.

The believers who so contended grew bold, and brought on a crisis of first rate importance, though very few seem to have recognized how important it was. Fortunately there was one man who did. Paul was a man of clear insight. He had faced problems for himself in the past, and he was just as ready to face problems for the Church now. He saw that if this contention were not met and silenced at once, the truths that were associated with the Messiahship of Jesus would be lost, and Christianity would become a sort of side issue of Judaism, and eventually be strangled. From the very beginning of the trouble he took a stand against the new movement.

It is well to realize the facts of the case. Jesus, the Apostles, and all the early believers were Jews. They assembled in the Temple and used its court for their preaching. What could be more reasonable than for Jewish Christians of Paul's day to note such customs, and in many cases to feel that they were in a way a part of Judaism ; separated from the Jews who remained in unbelief of Jesus, but still affected by the training of a lifetime ?

64

In Antioch it was quite different. The Church there was the largest outside Jerusalem, and it was largely, if not mainly, composed of Gentiles. The Jewish members of that Church would be Jews who had been brought up among Gentile surroundings, and had been compelled to mix with pagans in many of the activities of life. The definite separation between Jew and Gentile that marked the attitude of the Jews of Jerusalem and Judea had little place in Antioch, and Jews and Gentiles in the Church mingled freely in worship and in social intercourse. It was when some Christians from Jerusalem visited Antioch that trouble began to arise.

Before that time Peter had visited Antioch and had mixed freely with the Gentile believers there. When, however, some Christians from Jerusalem visited Antioch the situation was suddenly changed. It is said that they had come from James, that is, James the Lord's brother, though in view of what took place later, it is clear they were not acting in accordance with his instructions. Some of them were fervent members of the party that held strictly to the Mosaic Law, and adhered to its ritual ; to them circumcision was an all-important rite ; was it not the seal of the covenant God had made with Abraham ? No doubt they argued that Jesus was a Jew ; that he had been circumcised ; that he had kept the Law. Had he not said, " Think not that I came to destroy the Law " ?

The coming of these men caused a change

in the attitude of Peter ; he ceased to mix freely with Gentile Christians ; he " drew back " and separated himself. Of course he ought not to have done so, but Peter was subject to moments of weakness in the face of sudden difficulties. On this occasion, however, his action caused others to follow him, and even Barnabas wavered. It must have been a bitter moment for Paul. It was not an occasion when something could be passed over and put right later. The matter was too serious ; he must make an immediate, and an open stand. His own words set out the case : he went to Peter and " withstood him to the face " ; saying to him, " If thou, being a Jew, livest as do the Gentiles, and not as do the Jews, how compellest thou the Gentiles to live as do the Jews ? "

Peter accepted the rebuke, but his temporary defection, and the wavering of Barnabas, encouraged the Jews from Jerusalem to go further. They raised the whole question, saying of the Gentiles, " Except ye be circumcised after the custom of Moses, ye cannot be saved ". It was a direct challenge to the work Paul and Barnabas had been doing, and they took the lead in opposing the dangerous innovation. The Church at Antioch was deeply stirred, and after much discussion it was resolved to refer the matter to the apostles and elders at Jerusalem, and Paul and Barnabas, with certain others, were deputed to go as representatives of the Church.

There is no question about the views of the

Church at Antioch, for its members brought the deputation " on the way " towards Jerusalem. They passed through Phœnicia and Samaria, in both of which districts they were received with gladness, in fact " they caused great joy unto the brethren " ! There was no question as to the feelings of the Christians in both districts.

Before the meeting of the Church took place, Paul had an interview with Peter and others. It was a wise thing to do, for Peter and James exercised a great influence among the Palestinian Christians. Had Peter been an average individual it might have been thought that the rebuff he had received at Antioch would cause him to make things awkward for Paul. Peter was not a man of that type ; his lapses were always made good as soon as he recognized them ; it is this feature of his character that makes him such a lovable man.

One important side issue came out of this private meeting, for Peter and others requested Paul to persuade the Gentile Churches to make collections for the assistance of the poor in the Churches of Judea. Such a course was necessary because Jewish Christians could not expect to participate in any arrangements made by the priests for the help of the poor of the City and country.

A special meeting of the Apostles and elders followed. The purpose of the delegation was made known, and the point in dispute submitted. The meeting opened with a general discussion, in the course of which the matter was warmly debated. The "opposition" party submitted their contention that it was necessary for Gentile converts to be required to be circumcised, and to conform to the Law of Moses. Their arguments may be assumed to have been on the lines already suggested.

The chief interest centres in the addresses of the last four speakers. The first was Peter. It was appropriate that he should take a leading place in the matter, for he had been the one to " open the door of faith " to the Gentiles. He referred to that event, and said, " God, who knows the heart, bare witness to them, giving to them the Holy Spirit, as he also did to us ... purifying their hearts by faith ". Peter concluded with a pertinent question ; " Now therefore, why tempt ye God to put a yoke on the neck of the disciples, which neither our fathers nor we were able to bear ? "

Barnabas followed ; he had been in the Church in Jerusalem in the early days, and his words would help to prepare the way for Paul. Then Paul spoke. He told how the " door of faith " that had been opened by Peter had been flung open, as it were, in their experiences. An account of the journey he and Barnabas had made was his contribution to the discussion. They had not preached circumcision, but the grace of God had followed them, and was to be seen in the results that followed their efforts, for God had shown His approval by the gift of the Holy Spirit to Gentile believers. There could be no answer to such an argument.

James, the brother of Jesus, brought the discussion to an end. He enforced what he had to say by a quotation from Amos. Perhaps as one reads it in its original setting it will not seem to have much bearing on the matter that was being discussed. Yet it certainly implied that something of the nature of what had happened would have to take place, for it referred to Gentiles upon whom God's name was to be called. As the head of the Church in Jerusalem, James gave his judgment. Gentiles who turned to God were not to be troubled about questions of the Law, or the rite of circumcision. All that was necessary was that they should observe four things :

1. Abstinence from idolatry and its pollutions,
2. Abstinence from fornication,
3. Abstinence from partaking of things that had been strangled ;
4. Abstinence from eating blood.

A reason was given for the third and fourth items : " For Moses from generations of old hath in every city them that preach him, being read in the synagogues every Sabbath ".

It may seem strange that it should have been thought necessary to include item No. 2. We may be thankful that we live in different times. In the first Century worship in pagan religions regarded certain forms of fornication as a part of religion. It sounds horrible to us ; but it was looked upon as quite reasonable then. That such a change has taken place in public opinion is one of the blessings we owe to the Christian religion ; one of its greatest principles is purity.

In a sense the decision was a compromise, but it saved the situation, and prevented Christianity becoming gradually a form of Judaism. It was only an interim policy intended to bridge over the time till the Gentile element became an overwhelming influence in the Christian community. In later years Paul said nothing about the last two items ; he quietly dropped them, but in doing so he established a principle that applies not only to matters of eating and drinking, but to every action in human lives. Here are his words ; they are worthy of being carefully noted. " For if because of meat thy brother is grieved, thou walkest no longer in love. Destroy not with thy meat him for whom Christ died ... Overthrow not for meat's sake the work of God." That is true Christian charity, and should be the guiding principle with all who aim to live in Christ.

The outcome was the issue of a decree for the guidance of Gentile Churches. It read as follows :

"The apostles and the elders and brethren unto the brethren which are of the Gentiles in Antioch and Syria and Cilicia, greeting. Forasmuch as we have heard that certain which went out from us have troubled you with words, subverting your souls ; to whom we gave no commandment ; It seemed good unto us, being come to one accord, to choose out men and send them unto you, with our beloved Barnabas and Paul, men that have hazarded their lives for the name of our Lord Jesus Christ. We have sent therefore Judas and Silas, who themselves also shall tell you the same things by word of mouth. For it seemed good to the Holy Spirit, and to us, to lay upon you no greater burden than these necessary things ; that ye abstain from things sacrificed to idols, and from blood, and from things strangled, and from fornication ; from which if ye keep yourselves, it shall be well with you ".

Paul might well be content with the result. Although the matter had arisen out of events at Antioch, it was one of the most important conflicts that ever arose in the Christian Church. For all future time it prevented the Church ever being regarded as a part of the Jewish religion ; the Christians were seen to be a new community.

It was a definite victory for Paul and for freedom. It will be noticed that it was addressed only to the churches in Antioch, Syria, and Cilicia ; districts that were within comparatively easy reach of Jerusalem. It was not addressed to Christians outside those areas, though by the time the letter was issued there were plenty of Christians in other places, such as Galatia. True Paul delivered copies of the decree to the Churches of Galatia ; perhaps he foresaw the trouble that afterwards arose in that region. For the moment all was well ; he had gained the acceptance of the position for which he had fought, and was supported in his contention by the Apostles and elders of the mother Church in Jerusalem. No wonder that when the epistle was read to the assembly of the Church in Antioch, the members rejoiced for the consolation.

Unfortunately, though defeated, the opposition party was not silenced. They became bitter enemies of Paul, following him in his travels, and doing what they could, sometimes with unlooked for success, to raise the feelings of the believers against him and the principles for which he stood. They will be heard of again before long.

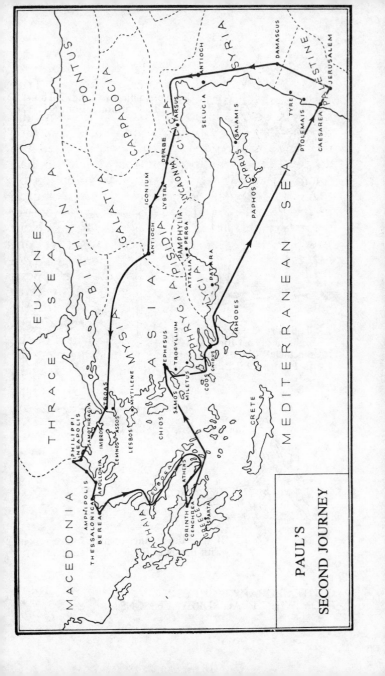

PAUL'S
SECOND JOURNEY

Roman soldiers (see e.g. 2 Tim. 2:4) and their armour (Eph. 6:11-17)

A Gladiator: The apostles were as gladiators set forth as a "spectacle" (the original word in 1 Cor. 4:9 is "theatre")

"If after the manner of men I have fought with beasts at Ephesus" (1 Cor. 15:32)

CONTEMPORARY FIGURES
FROM WHICH PAUL DREW LESSONS

CHAPTER IX

PAUL REACHES EUROPE

AFTER the issue of the decree referred to in the previous chapter, there was a time of quiet, marked by the peaceful growth of the Church. This was particularly noticeable in the Church at Antioch, now strengthened by the presence of Judas and Silas. Later Judas returned to Jerusalem, but Silas stayed to help in the work.

Although this work was important it did not satisfy Paul. He realized that he had a message for Gentiles further afield, and though his surroundings in Antioch were pleasant, and the fellowship of so many helpers agreeable, he desired to go to the " regions beyond ", a desire which carried his mind, though not, so far as is known, his presence, as far as Spain.

For the moment, however, he was content to make a much more modest proposal, and suggested to `Barnabas that they should revisit the places where they had proclaimed the Word, and see how the communities they had established were progressing. The proposal shows the solicitude of the Apostle for those who had learned the Truth through his instrumentality. Barnabas was quite willing, and suggested that they should take Mark with them again. Paul could not overlook Mark's departure from Asia Minor when he himself had been overtaken by a serious illness, and would not agree to his being included in the party. Barnabas insisted, and the contention became so sharp between the two friends that in the end they parted company, Barnabas taking Mark, who was related to him, and going to Cyprus. Paul chose Silas as his companion. and revisited Syria and his native province of Cilicia.

Nothing would be gained by attempting to apportion the blame for the quarrel. Both were men subject to human passions and prejudices. It is best to remember that the difference of ideas did not finally embitter the relations of the two men, and to note that Mark was restored to Paul's confidence before the end of his story is reached.

Paul and Silas left Antioch with the commendation of the brethren there. Avoiding the sea route this time they went through Syria and Cilicia, passing through the Cilician Gates, one of the narrowest passes in the world, where the walls of rock tower hundreds of feet above the traveller, and so reached Derbe and Lystra.

Lystra was the home of Timothy. Paul must have noted him in the past ; now he found that the promise of earlier times had not failed. Timothy was well versed in the Scriptures, and well reported of by the brethren of those parts. As Paul talked to him, and watched him performing his duties, he saw in him one who would be useful as a minister, qualified to occupy the position Mark was intended to occupy on his first adventurous journey. Timothy was ready. It was a great undertaking for so young a man. Paul probably told him of John Mark's failure in the past, and of the difficulties he was likely to meet. Timothy was prepared to face them, and submitted to the rite of circumcision.

The action of Paul in circumcising Timothy may seem strange, especially as he was carrying the decree which for ever freed Gentile converts from the obligations of the Mosaic Law. Timothy, however, was half a Jew, and the journey was to be made in harmony with the principle " to the Jew first ". Paul knew enough of the attitude of the Jews to realize the result that was likely to follow if he took an uncircumcised Jew into a Jewish synagogue. One of the principles that guided him in his dealings with various people was to be " all things to all men " ; a principle which he said he adopted " for the gospel's sake ".

Paul's action in this matter illustrates the real greatness of the man ; a little man would have been afraid of being accused of inconsistency in his actions regarding Titus and Timothy. Inconsistency is a charge few men are prepared to face ; he is a great man who, holding fast to principles, is not afraid of being misjudged. There are plenty of little men in the world, but the truly great have always been few.

It must have been with some feelings of sadness that Timothy said farewell to his mother and grandmother. He was going right away ;

it might be months, or even years, before he saw them again, but he was buoyed up by the thought that he had been chosen to be the minister, and the confidant, of such a man as Paul.

When Paul and his companions left Lystra everything seemed to go wrong. They passed through the cities of the district, leaving copies of the Jerusalem decree, and speaking words of exhortation so that the brethren might be established in the faith. When they left Iconium, the last of these cities, there was a choice of routes. They might go to Perga and return direct to Antioch, or they might seek further fields of activity. They chose the latter ; the road to the west called Paul, the road that led to Ephesus. He felt constrained by some unseen force, yet he was " forbidden " to preach in Asia (that is, the Roman province of Asia, a district of Asia Minor, bordered by Bithynia, Galatia, and Pisidia). Paul's intention seems to have been to go direct to Ephesus, the capital of Asia, travelling by the main road to that city. The time for this work had not come, and, forbidden to go there, they made their way to a point over against Mysia, intending to go to Bithynia. Their route was again overruled, and they ultimately arrived at Troas, between two and three hundred miles away from Timothy's home, and nothing had as yet been done by them. Whether the influence that controlled their route was direct or indirect is not clear ; it may have been a combination of both. They were subject to Spirit guidance ; the work they had to do was before them, and natural causes, as we deem them, can be so manipulated by God to cause His intentions to be carried out. It was so in this case ; a door was to be opened for a new and great work.

It certainly had not been a promising beginning, and Paul may have wondered if he had taken the right course in parting from Barnabas. At Troas all was made clear. One day during their stay there they met Luke. The meeting is not mentioned anywhere, yet it was a most fortunate one, for it led ultimately to the gospel of Luke being written, a book which has been described as " the most beautiful short story in the world ", also the Acts of the Apostles, the only biography we have of Saul, who is also called Paul. It had another result, equally unforeseen.

One night in Troas Paul lay awake wondering what they were to do ; ultimately he fell asleep and dreamed. Such an experience had shaped his course before ; it was to do so now. Luke, who was a man of Philippi, had probably spoken about his city, and now, in his dream Paul saw, and heard, a man of Macedonia, in which Philippi was situated. The words that reached his ear were, " Come over into Macedonia and help us ". Paul saw in this the reason for the interferences that had caused their alterations of route. There was no more hesitation ; no more trying to go one direction and then another. As Luke writes, " Straightway *we* sought to go into Macedonia, concluding that God had called *us* for to preach the gospel unto them ".

The change from the third person to the first is significant. It was " Paul ", " him ", and " he " ; now it is " we " and " us " ; Luke had joined the little band. Remember, Paul had been forced to go to Troas ; it was not the route he had purposed to travel, so the meeting was not prearranged. Luke was a doctor, " the beloved physician ", and as such would be a great help to a man like Paul, subject to attacks of illness from time to time.

Philippi was a leading city of Macedonia ; it was also a Roman colony. The population was made up of Greeks and Romans, with a small number of Jews. The Jews were so few in number that there was no synagogue in the city, and it was their custom to meet for worship by the river side in a *Proseuche*, that is, a place of prayer ; probably, but not necessarily a building used for that purpose. On their first Sabbath in Philippi Paul and his friends made their way to the riverside, hoping to find a meeting in progress. There was one, though it was only attended by women, but Paul and the others sat down and spoke to them.

Among those who listened was a woman named Lydia, a seller of purple. She was of Thyatira, a city of Asia ; she was therefore of the very province in which Paul had been forbidden to preach. She was probably a widow, and the head of a household. Thyatira was noted for its dyes, and Lydia traded in them, and, probably in purple dyed garments. She was well off, and was either a convert to the Jewish religion, or had been much attracted to it. Now she listened intently to what Paul had to say. The meetings must have continued week after week, and ultimately Lydia's heart was " opened " by the Lord, and she, with the members of her household, was baptized. Having thus joined the Christian community she invited Paul and his companions to take up their abode in her house. At first Paul declined ; it was a principle with him not to accept hospitality from his converts, lest it should cause any to think that he was actuated by a desire to be supported by those to whom he spoke. In this case Lydia made a personal matter of it, saying, " If ye have judged me to be faithful to the Lord, come into my house, and abide there ". Having profited from their spiritual things, she " constrained " them to accept her hospitality as a slight return.

The work by the riverside continued, and one day, as Paul and his friends were on their way to the *Proseuche* a young woman cried after them. She was possessed of " a spirit, a Python " ; so the Greek expresses it ; she was also a ventriloquist. Her strange powers brought her owners—for she was a slave—much gain. It was that which led to the trouble that ensued.

Day after day she followed them crying, "These men, slaves of the God Most High, proclaim to us the Way of Salvation". She did not use that language because she had any knowledge of Christianity, for the title, "God the Highest" was well known and often used by the pagans of the time. Stones containing prayers for salvation were there by the roadside, though the meaning attached to that word by the Greeks was something very different from what it meant when used by Paul, and as readers of the Bible have come to understand it. The girl had probably heard Paul use the word, and in her weak mental state used it in the way she did.

The experience was very annoying to Paul. He was in Philippi to make known the gospel of Christ with its message of eternal salvation, and he did not want the people of Philippi to identify that with the profit-making work of the Pythoness. He was "pained"—so the Greek implies. Turning round and facing the girl, he addressed the spirit that was supposed to be in her saying, in incisive tones, "I charge thee in the name of Jesus Christ to come out of her". The sudden command brought her to her senses, and the spirit "came out".

There is no more certain way to make men angry than to interfere with their profits. The owners of the girl, seeing their means of wealth spoiled, dragged Paul and Silas to the market-place, where they set them before the magistrates. They could hardly charge them with injuring their slave by giving her the proper use of her senses, and a more subtle charge had to be brought. They said, " These men, being Jews, do exceedingly trouble our city, and set forth customs which it is not lawful for us to receive, or to observe, being Romans ".

It was a very convenient charge to make against the two strangers. Roman Law was, in some ways, a model, but Roman Law as administered by some of the local officials was often very different. Roman writers have satirised the officious individuals who were praetors (or local magistrates) in provincial towns. They are described as " fussy ", and as exhibiting consequential airs. The propraetors of Philippi were men of this type, and the charge laid against Paul and Silas gave them just such an opportunity as they desired. It enabled them to show their importance. They made no pretence of hearing the case ; but commanded the lictors (that is, the sergeants or beaters) to tear the clothes from Paul's and Silas's backs, and to beat them with their rods.

Such beatings were carried out in public and were both humiliating and painful. Each blow drew blood, and when the beating was over the men were thrust into the inner prison, with their backs bleeding and their garments thrown over the oozing blood. By these means the propraetors upheld, so they thought, the dignity of Rome against the enemies of the Roman Empire !

Having received his charge, the gaoler took no chances ; he not only placed his prisoners in the inner prison, he also secured them by chains round their arms, and placed their feet in the stocks. He evidently thought they were dangerous criminals !

Some years afterwards Paul wrote to the Philippians, " Rejoice in the Lord always " ; yet it is not easy to picture two men with aching and bleeding backs, fettered, and fastened in the stocks, rejoicing and singing hymns unto God ; yet that is what Paul and Silas did at midnight. They sang some of the Songs of Zion. It may have been :

O praise the Lord, all ye nations ;
Laud him, all ye peoples ;
For his mercy is great toward us ;
And the truth of the Lord endureth for ever.
Hallelujah !

So unusual was the sound that the prisoners listened to them. And yet, how better could these disciples have occupied the time ? Sleep was impossible, and singing hymns, and praying to the God of all comfort, may have helped them to forget something of their sufferings and the humiliations they had endured.

Suddenly the silence, and the singing, were disturbed. An earthquake shook the foundations of the prison, the staples fell from the walls, the grip of the stocks was loosed, and the prisoners were free ! Probably the only reason why the prisoners did not take advantage of the offered freedom was the panic caused by the earthquake. The gaoler did not stay to think of this, or indeed, of anything except the charge he had received. If the prisoners escaped he would be held responsible ; that was his thought as he drew his sword to kill himself. He was stopped by the voice of Paul saying, " Do thyself no harm, we are all here ". So assured, he called for a light, " sprang " in (surely a sign of his excitement), trembling, and fell at the feet of Paul and Silas, crying, " Lords, what must I do to be saved ? " (The Greek uses the word *Kurioi*, the plural form of *Kurios*—Lord.)

What salvation had he in mind ? The Pythoness had cried, " These men proclaim unto you the way of salvation ". Was that in his mind ? or was it something of an even more worldly character, his safety in the circumstances that had arisen ? Whatever may have been in his mind, Paul gave it its highest meaning, and replied, " Believe on the Lord Jesus Christ, and thou shalt be saved, thou and thy house ".

Having made sure of his other prisoners, the gaoler took Paul and Silas, washed their stripes, listened to the word of the Lord as Paul expounded it, and then, with his household, was baptized. Their roles were now reversed ; the gaoler sat, metaphorically, at the feet of Paul who was still his prisoner. It is a thrilling story, yet it is only one among many in Paul's career.

Next morning there was a further change in the situation. According to a note in one old manuscript, the praetors were afraid that the earthquake had taken place because of the Divine displeasure at the illegalities of the previous day. Superstition was rampant in those times, and they felt uneasy. After all, they had not tried the two men ! They did not even know who they were ! So now they sent a message to the gaoler telling him to let them go. He went to Paul and Silas, no doubt thinking they would be only too pleased to get away after the treatment they had received. He was mistaken ; Paul had the future to think of—not his own, but that of others. There were the makings of a Church in Philippi, and the petty rulers of the town had better be taught a lesson.

" They have beaten us publicly, uncondemned, men that are Romans, and have cast us into prison ; and now do they cast us out secretly ? Nay, verily, let them come themselves, and let them bring us out." That was Paul's answer, and it had the effect Paul designed. The praetors were afraid, terrified in fact ; their actions, taken so lightly a day earlier, might lead to their own undoing. Roman citizenship was not a thing to be lightly set aside. There was only one thing they could do. Abjectly enough they " came and besought them " and " brought them out " ; then they " asked them to go away from the city ". They had been taught a well deserved lesson ; their upstart pride had been brought to shame. There can be no doubt the lesson helped the little Church that was established in the city.

Paul and Silas made their way to the house of Lydia, where they saw the brethren, comforted them, and left the city with sore backs, and with their faces to the West. Luke did not accompany them ; he stayed to carry on the work of evangelizing in the city, and of organizing the Church there. He did it so well that Paul speaks of him as one whose praise in the gospel was spread through all the Churches. Timothy also stayed behind.

CHAPTER X

IN THESSALONICA AND BEREA

PAUL'S departure from Philippi took place so suddenly that there was no time to arrange his next destination. As he and Silas left the city their thoughts were still westward, in which direction, something like a hundred miles away, was the city of Thessalonica. Two things probably influenced them to go there; first, there was a good road by which they could travel in comfort, and a number of Jews lived in the city, so that there would be a synagogue, in which they might expect to find an open door, at any rate for a time. They took up their quarters in the house of a Jew named Jason.

Thessalonica was one of the leading towns in the Roman Empire; it was a commercial centre, a feature which it still maintains under its modern name of Salonica. During their stay there they were helped with funds by the Church in Philippi, an assistance which Paul greatly appreciated. When he had occasion to write to the Church in Philippi some years afterwards, he made special mention of the help they had sent him, saying, " When I departed from Macedonia, no church had fellowship with me in the matter of giving and receiving, but ye only ". They had helped him on his journey, and after his arrival in Thessalonica they sent to him " once and again ". This help was supplemented by Paul's own labours, as he reminded the believers in Thessalonica, " Ye remember, brethren, our labour and travail ; working night and day that we might not burden any of you, we preached unto you the gospel of God ". Paul would not have it said of him that he made a living from his preaching !

There seem to have been special reasons why he adopted this attitude in Thessalonica. Later on, when he found it necessary to send letters to the Church there, he said, " Study to be quiet, and to do your own business, and to work with your hands ". " Now we command you, brethren, in the name of our Lord Jesus Christ, that ye withdraw yourselves from every brother that walketh disorderly . . . for we behaved not ourselves disorderly among you ; neither did we eat for naught at any man's hand, but in labour and travail, working night and day that we might not burden any of you." The moral of such references is obvious.

The hoped for open door presented itself, and for three Sabbaths Paul reasoned with the Jews and proselytes who attended the meetings in the synagogue, opening and alleging from their Scriptures that it was necessary for the Messiah to suffer, to die, and to be raised from the dead, and that Jesus of Nazareth was the Messiah.

It was a strange doctrine to them, but, like Jesus when speaking to his disciples after his resurrection, Paul showed how all things must needs be fulfilled which were written in the Law of Moses, and the Prophets, and the Psalms concerning the Messiah.

There was no lack of evidence to support his contention ; some of it plain, some in types and shadows. Taken as a whole, the evidence was overwhelming. In the Law there was the type of the lamb without blemish, offered every morning and evening. In the Prophets and the Psalms there were allusions to the Man of Sorrows, who was wounded for the transgressions of his people, and cut off from the land of the living. There was Messiah the Prince, cut off within the appointed period, yet not allowed to see corruption, but brought from the grave to the path of life to be crowned with glory and honour. There was the Sufferer crying, " My God, my· God, why hast thou forsaken me ? " whose hands were pierced, and his garments parted amongst others, through whom all the ends of the earth were to turn to the Lord, and worship before Him.

With testimonies like these, combined with the recital of his experiences on the road to Damascus, Paul preached Christ in the synagogue at Thessalonica, and as a result a number of his hearers were persuaded. When the use of the synagogue was denied the work was carried on elsewhere. He refers to it in the letters he sent to them later, wherein it is shown that the time spent there was one of labour and travail, preaching, exhorting, and setting an example of what a Christian life should be.

How long the work continued is not stated, but the account implies that it went on for some time, for, as already stated, the brethren in Philippi sent " once and again " to provide for his necessities.

As in other places the work there was brought to an end through the jealousy of the Jews. They gathered " certain lewd fellows of the baser sort ", as the Authorized Version calls them, and the Revised Version, " vile fellows of the rabble ", who set the city in an uproar. There was method in this. Among the lower classes the claims of the old pagan religions were strongest ; the upper classes were inclined to be sceptical. The Jews appealed to their fanaticism. At first they attempted to get hold of Paul and some of his helpers. Not finding them they laid hold of Jason and dragged him and certain others before the rulers of the city, crying, " These that have turned the world upside down are come hither also ; whom Jason hath received ; and these all act contrary to the decrees of Caesar, saying there is another king, one Jesus ".

The character of the charge suggests that the riot was more serious than the brief account in the Acts might seem to imply. That this was the case is probable from the language used in the letters to the Thessalonians, where Paul likens the action of the mob to that of the Jews, who

" both killed the Lord Jesus, and their own prophets, and drove us out ".   Persecution prepared to go to the length of killing had been practised among the Jews, and there would have been little point in making a comparison between that and the troubles in Thessalonica if the latter had been confined to what is recorded of a single occasion.

The charge suggests that considerable success had marked the efforts of Paul and Silas. They had turned the world upside down ! Allowing for the exaggeration that usually marks the sayings of the leaders of a disorderly mob, the words imply great results from the Apostolic preaching.   A few converts here and there could never be so described.   No wonder the Jewish authorities were envious ; they had never turned one single town upside down.

The accusation involved a capital charge. Another king had been announced. Understood as the common people were likely to do, it was treason, and it was imperative that the rulers of the city should take notice of it.

These rulers are, in the Greek, called *politarchoi*. No such title is found in the histories of the period, but a number of inscriptions have been found which refer to the supreme board of magistrates in Thessalonica by that title.   Fortunately these men were not easily impressed by a charge made by the leaders of a rabble. They listened to the charge and took a middle course ; they " took security " of Jason and certain others, and let Paul and Silas go. It was a course recognized by Roman Law.

The decision put an end to the actions of Paul and Silas in the city. To continue to work while Jason was subject to the "security" would have brought trouble on him, and Paul was not the kind of man to do that. He faced the inevitable, though he was sad as he and Silas left the city during the night. Timothy, who had rejoined them, stayed behind for a time to assist in the organization of the Church that had been formed.

Paul felt his separation from the Thessalonian believers very keenly. They were mostly Gentiles, for in a letter he wrote to them he speaks of how they turned to God from idols, to serve the Living and True God, and to wait for His Son from heaven. Paul longed to revisit them, but the " security " stood in the way. In his letter he wrote : " We, brethren, being bereaved of you for a short season, in presence, not in heart, endeavoured the more exceedingly to see your face with great desire, because we would fain have come unto you, I Paul, once and again, but Satan hindered us ". The words suggest an earnest desire to be with them. His work had been stopped just when he felt there was so much to be done.

" Satan hindered us ! " It may seem a strange way of accounting for his inability to return to Thessalonica. Who, or what, was the Satan ? It certainly was not the Satan of popular belief. It was not the rabble of Thessalonica that kept him away, though they had been opposed to him, and Satan means an adversary, or an opponent. Judging by the use of the term elsewhere it was the politarchs of Thessalonica in the exercise of their authority in taking " security " of Jason. They, by that action, prevented Paul from returning to the city. " This interpretation of the term ' Satan ' as denoting action taken by the governing power against the message from God, is in keeping with the figurative use of the word throughout the New Testament."[1]

Leaving Thessalonica the travellers still kept their faces westward until they arrived at Berea. This was a much less important place and they probably expected to be able to pursue their labours there undisturbed. Once more they made their way to the synagogue. After the persistent way in which the Jews had raised persecution against Paul in every city where he had preached the gospel, it might have been thought it was time to pass them by. It was no mere phrase, however, that he wrote to the Romans, " Brethren, my heart's desire and my supplication to God is for them, that they may be saved ", and he had " great sorrow and unceasing pain " as he experienced their rejection of his message.

On this occasion the result was in marked contrast to his experiences elsewhere. The Jews

---

[1]Ramsay : *Paul ; Traveller and Roman Citizen, p. 231.*

of Berea were " more noble " than those of other cities ; they heard him gladly, and searched the Scriptures daily, to see if the things he proclaimed were in accord therewith. The result was that many of them became believers, including a number of Greek ladies of good position, and also some men.

Then Jewish animosity broke out once more. News of what was happening reached Thessalonica, and Jews from that town came to Berea and stirred up the multitude against Paul. As before, they found the lower type of men more amenable to their influence. Paul had no desire for martyrdom ; there was too much work to be done, so he left the city. He had been foremost in the work, and the opposition was mainly directed against him. He went, accompanied by certain disciples, leaving Silas and Timothy behind to establish the believers in the faith.

Paul found a ship sailing for Athens. He and his friends went on board and sailed to that city. There he bade them farewell, and they returned to Berea with a message from Paul to Silas and Timothy to join him there as soon as they could.

CHAPTER XI

ALONE IN ATHENS

It seems that Timothy lost no time in following Paul to Athens, but on his arrival his leader was so anxious about the believers he had left in Thessalonica that he was sent back to that city to comfort them concerning their faith, and to reassure them of Paul's welfare. It was a clear indication of the consideration for others that characterized him ; he would rather be left alone in Athens than have the brethren in Thessalonica wondering how he was, and grieving over him. He says himself that he could no longer forbear ; he desired to know how they stood.

Alone in Athens ! There were crowds of people in the streets, men of many races and various beliefs, but there was none to greet the Apostle, or give him a word of cheer. The sense of being alone is never so keen as when one is alone amid crowds of people. No wonder Paul longed for the company of Silas and Timothy.

To many people the name of Athens recalls memories of some of the most interesting people in Grecian history. To others it suggests thoughts of Socrates and Plato, and various schools of philosophy. But whatever interest may be felt in some of these people, the one thing of enduring interest is the visit to the city of a Jew who proclaimed to some of its inhabitants the truth concerning " The Unknown God ".

Fully to appreciate the story of Paul's short stay in Athens it is desirable to have some idea of the city and the activities of its citizens. As the traveller approached the city itself, evidences of the worship of its people were seen. By the gate there was a building in which the vestments of the devotees of Minerva were kept, an image of Neptune, and a temple dedicated to Ceres. Just beyond the gate were more statues, including those of Apollo, Zeus, and Mercury, and a temple dedicated to Bacchus. In the Agora of the city, called the market-place in our Bibles, there were more statues, representing others of the gods of Greece. North of the Agora was the Areopagus—or Mars Hill, where a council of citizens used to meet—and yet more shrines. The people of Athens were not content with recognizing these supposed deities in this way, they also erected altars to abstract ideas, such as Pity, Fame, and Modesty. The outstanding feature of the place was the Acropolis, a rock about 150 feet high, which has been described as a " museum of art, of history, and of religion ". On it was a vast collection of beautiful architecture and sculpture, dedicated to the national glory and the worship of the gods. Overshadowing all was the Parthenon, a magnificent building, the temple of Athena, the patron goddess of the city. It was probably the most beautiful building in the world at that time. Its walls were adorned with sculptures and realistic figures representing various phases of the procession at the great festival that took place when the games were held in the district.

This brief account of the city and its surroundings will help the reader to appreciate the thoughts that filled the mind of Paul as he walked about, longing for the return of Timothy. His spirit was provoked as he saw the whole place given up to idolatry. Though he was only there waiting for his friends to come, he could not restrain himself.

There was a synagogue in which he was able, to some extent, to give voice to his feelings, though the Jews whom he met were probably so used to the sights of the city that they scarcely noticed the evidences of idolatry. Though they worshipped the One God, they had become accustomed to seeing images on every hand. With Paul it was different. When he was in the synagogue he might forget the idolatry of the Greeks as he " reasoned " with the Jews and the devout person who worshipped with them, but as soon as he went outside, there were the indications of idolatry on every hand.

As he walked through the Agora, he spoke to such people as would listen to him. Among those he met in this way were members of the philosophic sects of the city, including Epicureans and Stoics. The Epicureans taught that the gods were too remote from men to trouble about them, and that the best use of life was to get as much pleasure and enjoyment from it as was possible, though the pleasure and enjoyment were not simply, or even mainly, those afforded by indulgence in the lusts of the flesh ; they included intellectual pleasures also. The Stoics, on the other hand, believed in a divine government of the world, and taught a high standard of morality, but they associated this with the doctrine of a blind submission to the decrees of fate. The followers of this philosophy were no doubt satisfied with a much lower attainment than their leaders inculcated. Human nature seldom rises as high as its great teachers enjoin.

In conversation and discussion with these philosophers and their followers, Paul spoke of Jesus and the resurrection. To Greek philosophers Jesus was but a name ; a name which suggested nothing to them. As for resurrection, which they seem to have understood to be the name of a deity, that was no more intelligible than the other. Anastasis, the Greek word for resurrection, might be the name of a god, or rather of a goddess, but any idea of its real meaning was " to the Greeks foolishness ". They listened to Paul, and summed him up as a " babbler ".

What did they mean ? The Greek term they applied to Paul was a word of Athenian slang. Actually it meant a small bird that picked up seeds for its food ; in slang usage it was applied to one who picked up scraps rather than work for a living. As applied to Paul, it suggested one who picked up scraps of learning, a man filled with half-digested items of information, which he did not rightly understand, and which he passed on to his hearers with an air of superior knowledge. " An ignorant plagiarist ", is the definition that has been given to it as used in the Acts of the Apostles ; another is a " smatterer ".

The Agora was not a convenient place to discuss such matters, even with a " smatterer ", so some of the philosophers, or their followers, took hold of Paul and brought him before the Council of the Areopagus. There they asked him, " May we know what this new teaching is which is spoken of by thee ? " Never before had the Areopagus been the scene of such an enquiry. It was not a case of superstition versus superstition, or some matter of local interest ; it was Truth versus error, God or idols, Life or death.

Picture the scene. Paul, a Jew without a single sympathizer in the city, stands before the men who have described him as a " smatterer " ; around are the learned professors and lecturers of the university of Athens. It was a new situation for Paul. He had contended for the faith of Christ in Jewish synagogues ; he had faced a Gentile rabble more than once ; now he is to speak before the most learned assembly in the world, in the Oxford or Cambridge of the times. An ordinary man might have withdrawn ; Paul did not. He carried on in the spirit of one of his sayings, " I can do all things in him that strengtheneth me".

As on other occasions his address was a model, eminently suited to the assembly. It is one more illustration of what he meant when he said he was "all things to all men ".

The translation of the opening sentence as given in the Authorised Version makes Paul appear almost rude to his listeners, and Paul was never that. What he said, in effect, was, "Men, Athenians, in all things I perceive ye are somewhat superstitious (literally, very reverent to demons). For as I passed along and observed the objects of your worship I found also an altar with this inscription, TO AN UNKNOWN GOD. What therefore ye worship in ignorance, this set I forth unto you ".

This opening was calculated to arrest attention. Their admission that they did not know the God invited the disclosure that followed. That disclosure struck at the root of the whole system of Greek and Athenian worship. Paul went on, " The God that made the world, and all things therein, he, being Lord of heaven and earth, dwelleth not in temples made with hands ; neither is he served by men's hands, as though he needed anything, seeing he himself giveth to all life, and breath, and all things ; and he made of one every nation of men for to dwell on all the face of the earth, having determined their appointed seasons and the bounds of their habitation ; that they should seek God, if haply they might feel after him, and find him, though he is not far from each one of us ; for in him we live, and move, and have our being ; as certain even of your own poets have said, ' For we are also his offspring '. Being then the offspring of God, we ought not to think that the Godhead is like unto gold, or silver, or stone, graven by art and the device of man ".

In these few sentences the whole Greek worship of many gods was swept away. They had a god for everything ; a god of the earth and a god of the heaven ; a god of the sea and a god of the air ; a god of war and a god of peace. In striking contrast, The Unknown God proclaimed by Paul was One God, One only, and therefore supreme. Paul had a way of using his hands as he spoke, and we may imagine him pointing to the temples and statues as he declared that the God who made the world did not dwell in temples made with hands, and that He was not like to graven images.

It will be noticed that Paul referred to poets—not to a poet. Two are known, Aretas and Cleanthes, and it is interesting to note that it is almost entirely due to a quotation by a Jewish " smatterer " that either of them is remembered today, for outside the readers of the New Testament, very few are acquainted with anything that either of them wrote. Here is a translation of the passage from Aretas, who, by the way, was a Cilician :

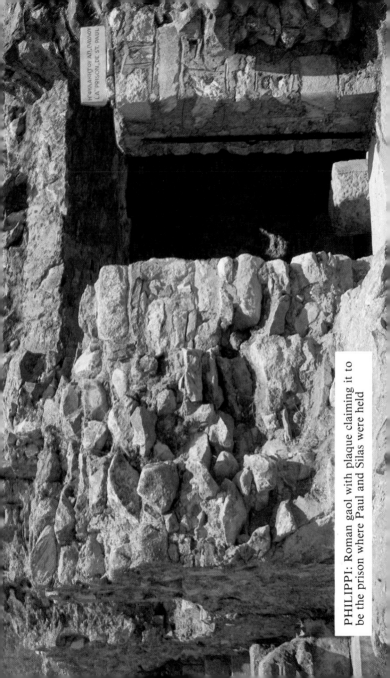

PHILIPPI: Roman gaol with plaque claiming it to be the prison where Paul and Silas were held

ATHENS: The Acropolis and remains of temples "made with hands"

From Zeus begin ; never let us leave
His name unloved. With him, with Zeus
    are filled
All paths we tread, and all the marts of
    men :
Filled, too, the sea, and every creek and bay ;
And in all things need we help of Zeus,
For we too are his offspring.

In Cleanthes the passage quoted reads :
Thou, who amid the Immortals art throned
    in highest glory,
Giver and Lord of life, who by law disposest
    of all things,
Known by many a name, yet One Almighty
    for ever,
Hail, O Zeus, for to thee should each mortal
    voice be uplifted ;
Offspring are we too of thine, we and all
    that is mortal around us.

Having brought his hearers to this point,
Paul raised the question of their relationship
to the commands of God. " The times of ignorance ", he said, " God overlooked, but now he
commandeth men that they should all everywhere
repent, inasmuch as he hath appointed a day
in which he will judge the world in righteousness
by the man whom he hath ordained, whereof
he hath given assurance unto all men, in that he
hath raised him from the dead ". Thus, for the
second time, human responsibility to God was
emphasized in addresses to Gentiles. First it

was made known to the rude and simple-minded Lycaonians of Lystra ; now it is announced to the educated Athenians. It is therefore a principle of universal application.

Imagine the feelings of those philosophers and professors of Athens ! " Times of ignorance indeed ! " Had this strange Jew come among them to charge them with ignorance ? The idea was preposterous. And what did he wish them to believe ? The strangest fancy possible—a dead man raised to life, and who was to become the ruler of mankind ! What a notion !

The idea of Jesus Christ being raised as an assurance that God would judge the world in righteousness was too much for these philosophers. It was something new to them, and though it was one of their chief occupations in life to tell, or to hear, of some new thing, they wanted no more. Some mocked ; others put the matter aside, saying they would hear Paul again at some other time ; and there the matter ended.

Paul was disappointed. The address which had been excellently reasoned out had failed. It had been spoken in surroundings that should have caused it to arrest attention ; yet the result is summed up in these words, " Then Paul went out from among them. But certain men clave unto him, and believed ; among whom also was Dionysius, the Areopagite, and a woman named Damaris, and others with them ". These " clave " to him, and to them he made known the love of God, and faith in Christ, the Saviour of men.

This visit to Athens had a great effect upon Paul. It made him realize more than ever that " not many wise after the flesh, not many mighty, not many noble are called ". Henceforth he determined to adopt a simple style ; to speak to the hearts of his hearers as he unfolded the gospel message in the simplicity it required.

CHAPTER XII

AT WORK IN CORINTH

PAUL left Athens disappointed and anxious; disappointed because his work there had not been a success, anxious concerning the welfare of the believers in Thessalonica. He was uncertain what to do. Finally he went down to the port where he found a ship sailing for Cenchrea, the port for Corinth. He boarded her, and was soon in Corinth.

Corinth, the capital of the province of Achaia, was a very different kind of place from Athens. The latter was a place of learning, Corinth was a busy centre of merchandise, and very populous. It was notorious for the wealth and for the vices of its inhabitants, who seem to have partaken of the evils of the various nationalities that thronged its streets and marts. It was the place where what were known as the Isthmian games took place, not in the city itself, but at a spot a short distance to the north-east. In these games there were contests of various kinds, including foot- and chariot-racing, wrestling and boxing ; men fought with wild beasts and with each other. The prizes awarded to the victors were wreaths cut from a tree in a sacred grove near by. These games provided a number of allusions and illustrations mentioned in the letters Paul subsequently wrote to the Church of Corinth.

When Paul arrived in the city he was depressed in mind and body. He says of himself " I was with you in weakness, and in fear, and in much trembling ". It is quite understandable ; he had been driven from city after city ; his experiences at Athens had been disappointing, and he had been alone ! Better things, however, were in store.

Paul's first experience in Corinth was an earnest of those better things. Going through one of the streets of the city he saw a man weaving tent-cloth ; he was a Jew named Aquila, who, with his wife Priscilla had come to reside in the city. It was a happy meeting, for the three became lifelong friends. At first they were attracted to each other by their community in trade, and Paul arranged to stay with them. Whether Aquila and Priscilla were already Christians we do not know ; if they were not they soon became such, and remained faithful throughout the whole of Paul's life.

Aquila and his wife had come from Rome ; they had been forced to leave that city by an Imperial decree banishing Jews from the capital, though a Roman historian says it was difficult to keep Jews out of that city because of their numbers. Aquila was one of those who left, though later he and his wife returned to Rome.

Although Paul settled down with them in Corinth he was anxious about Silas and Timothy,

and his converts in Thessalonica. As he and
Aquila sat at their work day by day the conversation must often have been about them. Aquila,
on the other hand, would speak of the greatness
of Rome with its teeming population, and it may
be it was because of this association of Paul with
Aquila that, a little later, Paul said, " After I
have been there (Jerusalem) I must also see
Rome ".

The principal topic of conversation, however,
must have been the subject of Paul's preaching—
Jesus Christ. Every Sabbath he was in the
synagogue reasoning with Jews and Greeks,
" not with excellency of speech, or of wisdom ",
as he afterwards said, but in demonstration
of the Spirit and of power. He had tried the
former at Athens, and it had been a comparative
failure, so now in Corinth he determined " not
to know anything among them save Jesus Christ
and him crucified ".

One day while Paul was engaged in these
labours Silas and Timothy arrived in the city.
They probably found where he was by enquiring
at the synagogue, and at once sought him out.
It must have been a joyful meeting ; one of the
bright spots in Paul's life. Their arrival allayed
one of Paul's anxieties. When they told him
about the brethren in Thessalonica another
anxiety disappeared. Ever since he had left
their city he had been praying for their welfare ;
now he heard good news of them, though the
good was mixed with tidings of suffering and

persecution. The troubles that had driven him from their city had overtaken the Christians, so that they suffered the same things of their own countrymen as did the Churches of Judea from the Jews.

Various emotions stirred Paul as he listened to the reports of Silas and Timothy. If it had been possible he would have gone back to Thessalonica immediately, but that was impossible ; " Satan " still hindered him. Besides, there were indications that there was a great work to be done in Corinth. In the circumstances he did the next best thing—he wrote a letter to them.

When Paul began to dictate that letter he was doing something much greater, and more important, than he imagined. His object was to encourage the believers in Thessalonica ; what he did was to *begin to write the New Testament*. The very first words of that book ever written were, " Paul, and Silvanus, and Timothy, unto the Church of the Thessalonians, in God the Father, and the Lord Jesus Christ ; grace to you and peace ". What words they are ! In God ! In Christ ! grace and peace ! Read that letter ; read it carefully, for it is unique.

Paul did not write the letter himself ; he dictated it, perhaps, to Timothy, though Paul added the final words. A more striking example of this practice will be seen in another letter— the second to Thessalonica, where he wrote,

" The salutation of me Paul with mine own hand, which is the token in every epistle ; so I write ".

One theme that enters into the letter is that Christ is coming. The Thessalonians turned to God from idols, to " wait for his Son from heaven ". They were to be Paul's crown of glorying " before our Lord Jesus Christ at his coming ". He prayed that their hearts might be kept unblameable in holiness " at the coming of the Lord Jesus ". Comforting them concerning some of their number who had died, he told them how the Lord " shall descend from heaven . . . and the dead in Christ shall rise ". His final prayer for them was that their " spirit and soul and body be preserved entire, without blame, at the coming of our Lord Jesus Christ ".

As one reads the letter a spirit of gladness will be found to run through it. " We give thanks to God for you all." " We thank God without ceasing." " What thanksgiving can we render again unto God for you for all the joy wherewith we joy for your sakes before our God ? "

The messenger who took the letter to Thessalonica returned to Paul with news of an unforeseen result it had produced on some of the believers there. They gave a literal meaning to Paul's words about " we who are alive, that are left unto the coming of the Lord ", and expected that event to take place almost at once. Some of them ceased to work ; what was the good of working if the Master was soon to return ? So Paul wrote another letter in which, after commending their faith and love, he told them of certain developments that must take place before Christ returned. They should have known this, as he said : " Remember ye not that when I was yet with you, I told you these things ? "

Such matters must be left for other treatment ; they do not bear directly on the life of Paul. It will be sufficient here to emphasize the points that bore on the conduct of the believers of the day. They were to withdraw from those who were disorderly ; to imitate him in the example he had set in " not eating bread for naught " ; he had worked day and night that he should not be a burden to them. He laid down the principle that " if any will not work, neither let him eat " !

Writing letters did not interfere with the work in hand in Corinth. " Constrained by the word ", Paul testified to the Jews that the crucified Nazarene was the Christ. It was of little avail ; the great majority opposed and blasphemed, until Paul shook out his clothes, as if to shake off the dust of the synagogue, saying, " Your blood be upon your own heads ; I am clean ; henceforth I will go unto the Gentiles ". He gave up preaching in the synagogue and commenced to teach next door, in a house belonging to a proselyte named Titus Justus. It looked as if there was a complete break between Paul and the Jews ; the very nearness of his meeting place and the synagogue must have seemed to emphasize it.

It must have caused an immense sensation among the Jews, and may be, among the Gentiles as well, when Crispus, the ruler of the Synagogue, applied for baptism into Christ. How important an event it was is shown by the fact that Paul departed from his usual practice of allowing his assistants, Silas or Timothy, to administer the ordinance of baptism, and undertook the duty himself.

The shock to the Jews caused by this happening must have been great. They immediately appointed a successor to Crispus, Sosthenes by name, and it must have been a still greater shock when a little later he too joined the Christians, for it seems fairly certain that the Sosthenes who joined Paul in the salutation to the Church at Corinth was he. Paul would hardly have singled him out for special mention if he were not well known to them.

Among the Gentile population the work prospered exceedingly, though not without serious opposition. Something of this opposition is suggested by some words in the letter to the Thessalonians, which was written from Corinth. " Pray for us ", Paul wrote, " that the word of the Lord may run and be glorified, even as also it is with you, and that we may be delivered from unreasonable and evil men."

In a vision which he had about this time he was told that God had much people in the city, and that he was not to be afraid. For eighteen months the work went on, not only in Corinth but in the district of Achaia.

At the end of eighteen months Jewish animosity flared up in an endeavour to frustrate the work. A new proconsul came to Achaia, Gallio, a brother of the philosopher Seneca. He was a man of a mild and gentle disposition ; his brother said of him, " No mortal man is so sweet to his dearest love as Gallio is to all mankind ".

The Jews probably thought it would be easy to influence such a man, so they brought Paul before his judgment seat on a charge that he persuaded men to worship contrary to the law. They met with a decided rebuff. Gallio seems to have taken some steps to enquire into the allegations made, and when Paul would have spoken in his defence, Gallio stopped him, saying, " If it were a matter of wrong, or of wicked villany, O ye Jews, reason would that I should bear with you ; but if they are questions about words and names, and your own law, look to it yourselves ; I am not minded to be a judge of these matters ". Something like contempt seems to have moved him in the matter, for he " drave " them from the judgment seat. He may have been influenced by the fact that the Jews had been driven from Rome by Imperial decree.

This attempt of the Jews to put a stop to the work recoiled on their own heads. They were never popular among Greeks and Romans, and feeling often ran strongly against them. Their aloofness naturally influenced the people against them, and on this occasion the people of Corinth took the part of the witnesses for the Truth. They got hold of Sosthenes, the ruler of the synagogue, and beat him before the judgment seat, apparently in the presence of Gallio himself. But Gallio " cared for none of these things ".

The attempt to stop the preaching of the gospel in Corinth, and the ignominious failure of the Jews to do so, led to new interest in the teaching of Paul.   A little excitement often attracts attention to a cause. Paul stayed there for some time longer, defined as " yet many days ", after which he took his departure, and sailed for Syria, accompanied by Aquila and Priscilla.   At Cenchrea he sheared his head, having taken a vow.

A great work had been done in Corinth and the surrounding districts of Achaia, and a Church had been established. It was by no means an ideal church, and it caused Paul much concern, as will be seen later.

On their way to Syria Paul and his companions called at Ephesus where Aquila and Priscilla determined to stay ;   they may have been induced to do so by the fact that Ephesus was celebrated for the manufacture of tents. During a short stay Paul once more used the synagogue to reason with the Jews. He was not there long enough for the usual opposition to develop ; probably he only had time to touch upon the simplest matters. The Jews requested him to stay, but he refused, though he promised to visit them at a later date. He sailed from Ephesus to Caesarea, whence he journeyed to Jerusalem, and then to Antioch, which he regarded, naturally enough, as his headquarters.

CHAPTER XIII

TROUBLE IN GALATIA

WHEN Paul left Corinth it was his purpose to keep the Passover in Jerusalem. In some respects he was still a Jew, and conformed to the provisions of the Law, including its festivals, so long as those provisions did not compromise the freedom he saw enshrined in the Christian religion. Apparently he was delayed on the journey, for there is no indication that he kept the feast at this time. The record simply states that he went to Jerusalem, where he " saluted " the Church, and then passed on to Antioch, where he met old friends. No doubt he told them how things had gone while he had been on his journey. They would rejoice over his successes, and sympathize with him over the troubles that had followed, his disappointment at Athens, his troubles at Corinth. To them he would confide his hopes, especially the one that was developing in his mind, that he would be able to visit Rome.

During his stay in Antioch bad news reached him about the Churches in Galatia. The news may have come through Timothy, who would naturally keep up a connection with Lystra, where his mother lived. Perhaps Timothy took advantage of Paul's stay in Antioch to visit his home and kindred. While there he would hear of the state of the various Churches in Galatia. The news he brought back was serious. Members of the Judaizing party had been there. Though they had been beaten when the controversy came to a head at the Council of Jerusalem, they had not given way. For some reason or other Galatia seemed to be particularly responsive to their efforts, and it was obvious that, if the situation was to be saved, something would have to be done, and done quickly. At the moment Paul could not go to Galatia, though he made up his mind to do so at the earliest opportunity. The next best thing, as it had been in the case of Thessalonica, was to write them a letter. That letter was the one known as the Epistle to the Galatians.

To appreciate that letter it is useful to recall certain facts about the past. When Paul first arrived among the Galatians he was tired, ill, and suffering ; they, on the other hand, had been considerate, kindly, and helpful. In his letter he reminded them of these facts. " Ye know ", he wrote, " that because of an infirmity of the flesh I preached the gospel unto you the first time." He told them how they had received him " as an angel of God, as Jesus Christ ". Then they would have plucked out their own eyes and given them to him ! Now the people who had received him with so much consideration were listening to some who had come among them teaching a form of Judaized Christianity, and, what was worse, had received their teaching.

How deeply Paul was stirred by what had happened may be seen from the language of the letter he wrote, and some of the things said in it. " I marvel that ye are so quickly removing from him that called you in the grace of Christ unto a different gospel." " Even if we (i.e. Paul, Timothy, and Silas) or an angel from heaven should preach unto you any gospel contrary to that which we preached unto you, let him be accursed." " O foolish Galatians, who did bewitch you ? " Such expressions indicate the state of the Apostle's mind when news of the change reached him.

Contrary to his usual procedure Paul seems to have written this epistle himself. No one is associated with him in the opening phrases, nor in the final sentences. In the last chapter he says, " See with how large letters I have written unto you with mine own hand ". The general language, the strong expressions that are used, and the fact that he wrote it himself, show the extreme urgency of the position as it appeared to Paul.

No attempt can be made to give an exposition of this, or any other, epistle, but every reader will be well advised to read it through, having regard to the circumstances that caused it to be written. Note how Paul's feelings seem to get the better of him at times ; his changing moods and his forcible expressions. Note, too, the almost incoherent way in which, in the second chapter,

CORINTH: Remains of the temple of Apollo

EPHESUS: The theatre
"And the whole city was filled with confusion:
and having caught Gaius and Aristarchus, men of
Macedonia, Paul's companions in travel, they
rushed with one accord into the theatre"

(Acts 19:29)

he refers to Titus accompanying him on a visit
to Jerusalem.

A key-word of the letter is "freedom".
"With freedom did Christ set us free." "Stand
fast therefore, and be not entangled again in a
yoke of bondage." If they underwent the rite
of circumcision, they would lose this freedom
and be "debtors" to the whole Law.

Another feature that marks the letter may
be pointed out. Look at the impulsive words,
the arguments, the outpouring of the writer's
feelings, the curse (anathema) pronounced on
certain individuals, and then note the sudden
change that breaks over the letter as Paul wrote,
"The fruit of the Spirit is love, joy, peace,
longsuffering, kindness, goodness, faith, meekness, self-control ; against such things there is
no law " ! Sudden changes like this add to the
interest, and the effectiveness, of Paul's letters.

Having despatched this letter to the Galatians, Paul followed it up by a personal visit,
a visit which is summed up in a single verse :
"And having spent some time there (i.e. in
Antioch of Syria) he departed and went through
the region of Galatia and Phrygia, in order,
establishing the Churches ". That is all that is
said, but it will be seen from the Epistle to the
Galatians, that the Churches sadly needed
establishing in view of the attempts of the
Judaizers to interfere with the liberty to which
the gospel had called their members. Had the
Judaizers succeeded in their designs the history

of the Christian Church would have been altered. No one seems to have realized the gravity of the situation as clearly as Paul, and we may well thank God that such a man had been prepared with sufficient foresight, and sufficient pertinacity, to carry on the necessary work. Perhaps no incident in his career more effectually indicates what he meant by that clause of the Foreword which says, " Beside those things that are without, there is that which presseth upon me daily, anxiety for all the Churches ".

An incident that happened about this time should be mentioned here, although it is not directly concerned with the work of the Apostle. It will be remembered that when Paul was on his way to Jerusalem, he was accompanied as far as Ephesus by Aquila and Priscilla. They stayed at Ephesus, where they settled down. While they were in the city an Alexandrian Jew, named Apollos, came to the city. He was an unusually good speaker, and was " mighty in the Scriptures ", that is, in the Old Testament, for the New was not yet in existence. He was a disciple of John the Baptist, who had proclaimed the coming of the Messiah. It may seem strange that he had heard nothing of the mission of Jesus in Galilee and Judea, nothing about his death and resurrection. It should be remembered that he was a Jew of Alexandria. Jesus's disciples were almost entirely Galileans ; they were common people, fishermen and agriculturists, and artisans ; Apollos of Alexandria would be a learned man ; perhaps he had been associated with some of the great schools of the city.

Aquila and Priscilla heard him speaking in the synagogue at Ephesus. They invited him to their house, where they spoke to him, and told him of the great things which had taken place in connection with Jesus of Nazareth, of his mission as the Lamb of God who was to take away the sin of the world ; his death and resurrection. With his mind prepared by the teaching of John it took little effort to enable him to realize the additional truths that were necessary, and he became one of the most eloquent advocates of the Christian religion.

Apollos was only passing through Ephesus, and was on his way to Corinth, so the brethren in the former city wrote to the disciples of Achaia to receive him. There he proved to be a great help to the work in hand; for he powerfully confuted the Jews, proving out of their own Scriptures that Jesus of Nazareth was the Messiah.

As Apollos does not come into contact with Paul, it may be well to refer here to the only other allusion to him, particularly as it throws a good deal of light on the character of Paul, and of Apollos. When Apollos reached Corinth, his eloquence charmed some of the members of the Church there, and they began to look upon him as a leader. It has been pointed out that the Corinthian Church was by no means an ideal one. Schism divided it ; factions arose, and one of the parties used Apollos' name as a slogan, saying, " I am for Apollos ", while others adopted the names of Paul, Cephas (Peter) and Christ.

Later on Paul wrote a letter to them in which he pointed out the evils of schism. In a reference to Apollos in this connection he gave an excellent example of the spirit that characterized him. " As touching Apollos ", he wrote, " I besought him much to come unto you with the brethren, and it was not at all his will to come now, but he will come when he shall have opportunity." The reluctance of Apollos was evidently due to the use that had been made of his name. The whole incident reflects great credit on both Paul and Apollos. Paul had wrought long and sincerely for the brethren in Corinth, and found little gratitude, yet he does not show the slightest sign of jealousy at the regard shòwn for his fellow worker. On the contrary, he urged him to go to Corinth. As for Apollos, he obviously sought no glory as the leader of a faction, and purposely stayed away, thus doing what he could to arrest the schism that was working like leaven. Both men manifest the characteristic of self-effacement, a trait which is sometimes very difficult to manifest, and is not easy to carry out consistently.

During the special journey made to Galatia Paul made arrangements for regular collections to be made on behalf of the members of the Church in Jerusalem. It was a poor Church ; was it not James, the leader of it, that wrote,

" Did not God choose them that are poor in the world to be rich in faith ? " It is part of the fellowship of the gospel to minister to the necessities of the saints, for fellowship is a term that must not be confined to distinctly religious matters like the Breaking of Bread. The word means a partaking, whether it be the good things of the gospel or of the more lowly things of life.

Although the first idea of this collection dates back to the time of one of Paul's visits to Jerusalem, he does not seem to have taken any regular steps to put such a plan in operation. Paul was a man of acute sensitiveness, and seems to have been afraid of being regarded as a money-making preacher. From this time, however, the collection for the poor of Jerusalem seems to have become a regular thing.

CHAPTER XIV

WORK AND TROUBLE IN EPHESUS

AFTER his work on behalf of the Galatian believers Paul lost no time in carrying out his promise to return to Ephesus. At first he followed the great Roman road that led westward, then he turned and followed a shorter, but much rougher, route which took him through what Luke calls " the upper country ". He did it to reach Ephesus a little sooner, though by doing so he had to forego visits to Colosse and Laodicea.

It will be recalled that on his brief visit a little earlier, he was welcomed by the Jews of the city, and that he left Aquila and Priscilla there. They had now left, and had probably returned to Rome. Ephesus was the chief city of the province of Asia, with a haven on the sea coast ; it was also a principal seat of trade, with a system of roads leading in various directions.

In accordance with his usual practice Paul carried on his trade while he was there, for in a letter which he wrote while in Ephesus he says, " Even unto this present hour we both hunger and thirst, and are naked, and are buffeted, and have no certain dwelling place (a sure indication that Aquila and Priscilla had left the city) ; and we toil, working with our own hands ".

On his arrival in the city he found a number of disciples who, like Apollos, had been followers of John the Baptist. They had probably arrived after the departure of Aquila and Priscilla ; hence they remained in ignorance of the further truths concerning the Messiah. When Paul met them he asked if they had received the Holy Spirit when they believed. Their answer was, " Nay, we did not so much as hear whether the Holy Spirit was given ". Paul at once opened up the " things concerning the Name of Jesus Christ " to them, and they were baptized into the name of the Lord Jesus, after which Paul laid his hands upon them and they received the Holy Spirit.

For three months Paul carried on his work of preaching in the synagogue, reasoning and persuading the things concerning the Kingdom of God, and the things concerning Jesus of Nazareth. This soon proved unpalatable to the Jews ; they could not bring themselves to accept as a Messiah one who had become a curse by the manner of his death. Moreover, they saw the tendency of Paul's teaching, and the interest they had manifested on his first visit died away.

Some of them went further and adopted an attitude of opposition, speaking evil of " The Way", a term often applied to Apostolic teaching, for that teaching was not merely the proclamation of certain truths to be believed, but also of a way of life that must be followed by those who accepted the doctrines.

The time soon came when Paul saw that he would have to break away from the synagogue altogether, for the Jews began to adopt a violent attitude towards him. He referred to this in an address he delivered to the elders of the Church later on, when he reminded them that he had been among them with trials which befell by the plots of the Jews. With his companions and converts he removed to the school of one Tyrannus, where, between the hours of eleven and four, he was able to reason with all who would attend. He himself describes the opportunity thus afforded him as " a great door and effectual ", though " there were many adversaries ". For two years this went on, and all that dwelt in Asia heard the gospel story. It may be well to point out that " Asia " does not mean the continent known by that name today, but a Roman province in the west of Asia Minor.

Ephesus was a centre from which it was possible to carry on an extensive campaign in the war of Truth versus Error, or Christ versus the religions of Greece. The expression used above, " All they that dwelt in Asia ", may be a figure of speech, but it suggests a very great work, and the knowledge of Christ found its way among an ever increasing circle. In that work Paul and his helpers journeyed to various places embraced in the area to which the Seven Epistles in the Apocalypse were sent—the Seven Churches in Asia.

A less spectacular work was also going on, for Paul speaks of teaching from house to house. Nothing can better express the careful way in which Paul sought to make known the " unsearchable riches of Christ ". It is one thing to proclaim the Truth from a public platform ; it is quite another thing to go quietly from house to house, talking, reasoning, sometimes entreating, in an endeavour to bring men and women to Christ.

Other reasons also contributed to the success of the work. Miracles of a special kind were wrought ; handkerchiefs and aprons were taken from Paul to sick folk, and the sick folk recovered. Such miracles had a suitable place in the pioneering days, when the Apostles were proclaiming their extraordinary doctrine of a Christ who had been crucified and then raised to life again, and who was to be the Messiah of whom the Israelitish prophets had spoken. There is a special point about these miracles that is worthy of mention. The salvation set before men and women in the proclamation of the Apostles is itself a miracle (using that term as implying something beyond the ordinary " laws " of nature), so that it was something to which miracles might be a fitting witness. By the operation of natural laws, human nature, with its sin and frailty, cannot produce sinlessness and immortality, so that, apart from miracle, the end proclaimed by the gospel, eternal life, or a participation in the Divine nature, is impossible.

If, as some contend, miracles never happen, then sin must be eternal, so that the issue was sufficiently important to make miracles not only possible, but probable. A divine messenger in those days might reasonably be expected to produce some credentials of the divinity of his mission.

The effect produced by the miracles was increased by the futile attempts of others to imitate them. Ephesus was a centre for various kinds of magic, and the magical arts were studied and practised by both Jews and Gentiles. Among the former were the sons of one Sceva, a chief priest in the synagogue. Two of them essayed to cure a madman by adjuring the supposed " evil spirit " in the name of Jesus, to come out of him, but were so maltreated by the man that they had to flee, leaving their clothes behind them. The case became notorious, and this again reacted to the advantage of Paul and all that he stood for. According to the record, " The Name of the Lord Jesus was magnified ".

The combined result of the preaching, the miracle working, and the failure of others to imitate the latter, was that many who listened to the words of Paul gave outward indication of the effect produced upon them. Some had dabbled in the black arts, as they are sometimes called. When they accepted the simple truths taught by Paul, they brought the books which they had been studying, and which dealt with " curious arts ", and burned them. The value of this bonfire of magical books is said to have been fifty thousand pieces of silver.

As Paul's labours in Ephesus drew to an end he turned his attention to the future. There were Churches in Macedonia and Achaia which he had been instrumental in founding. What was happening to them? Were their members remaining faithful to the ideas he had proclaimed? He was anxious about them, as he well might be after his experiences in Galatia. He would have liked to visit them, and give them what help he could; then he would go to Jerusalem with the contributions of the Gentile Christians for the poor of that city. Then his mind took a further sweep, and he said to himself, "After that I must also see Rome!" For the time being, however, he was not ready to undertake such a journey, so he sent Timothy and one named Erastus to visit the Churches in Macedonia and Achaia, while he finished the work that was still to be done in Ephesus.

During the time Timothy and Erastus were away an incident occurred which caused him to leave Ephesus at once. Ephesus was devoted to the worship of Diana, the Artemis of the Greeks. A magnificent temple which had been erected to her honour in the city was regarded as one of the seven wonders of the world. The original temple had been burned down, but another had been built with even greater magnificence than before.

One outcome of this devotion of the people of Ephesus and of the adjoining districts to the worship of Artemis was that a great trade was done in the manufacture and sale of small shrines in her honour ; they were made of various metals, including silver, also of marble, terra cotta, and so forth. The purchasers of these shrines kept them in their houses, and buried them with their dead. Great numbers were presented to the goddess herself, or rather to priests who looked after her worship. These were kept in the temple, and from time to time those made of terra cotta, and others of small value, were cleared out to allow more room for further offerings. The manufacture and sale of these shrines constituted a valuable source of income to the merchants and workers of Ephesus.

There is no more effectual way of stirring up animosity than by interfering with a man's prosperity ; the pocket is a sensitive part of a man's interests. One of the people connected with the trade in shrines took the lead in an attempt to prevent Paul and the Christians doing anything further to interfere with it. Demetrius—that was his name—called the workmen together to confer on the best way to protect their interests. It was something like a Trade Guild meeting, and Demetrius took the chair. He showed considerable acumen in the way he handled the matter. Had he based his appeal solely on the question of loss of money it might have had less effect ; the public might have been quite unconcerned in a movement whose chief aim was to increase the money that was to be taken out of their pockets. Demetrius took another line, a line that was almost sure to have effect. Among the things he said was, " Not only is there danger that our business come into disrepute, but also that the temple of the great goddess Artemis be made of no account, and that she should even be deposed from her magnificence, whom all Asia, and all the inhabited earth worshippeth ".

That was an irresistible appeal to the people of Ephesus ; that touched them all, not the members of the Guild only, and a great shout went up—" Great Artemis of the Ephesians ". There was something very natural in this. The centuries seem to roll away, and one can almost think it is a modern crowd whose actions are being described. Give a crowd a slogan and it may do things that no one can foresee. At once the whole city was in confusion, and the people rushed into the theatre, shouting first one thing and then another, for most of them did not know what was the matter.

Two of Paul's companions were dragged into the theatre by some of the crowd. With characteristic fearlessness Paul would have followed them, but was persuaded by the brethren to keep away from these " wild beasts " of Ephesus. Their advice was supported by certain officers of the city, spoken of as Asiarchs, who were friendly to him. (The Asiarchs of Ephesus, ten in number, were chosen from among the wealthiest of the citizens. They were officials who acted as priests connected with the worship of the Emperor, and not the local deity, and this may account, to some extent, for the favour they showed Paul.)

In the absence of Paul the Jews put forward one Alexander. The sight of him beckoning with his hand for silence was sufficient. He was a Jew, and in Grecian cities like Ephesus the Jews were never popular. It was as a match to powder, and for two solid hours the crowd shouted out their slogan, " Great Artemis of the Ephesians ".

When the violence of the crowd had spent itself, and the Recorder was able to make himself heard above the tumult, he said, " Men, Ephesians, what man is there who knoweth not how that the city of the Ephesians is the temple-keeper of the great Artemis, and of the image that fell down from Zeus ? " This little flattery, followed by a cold douche of fact, stilled the meeting. He then pointed out that Paul and his companions were neither plunderers of temples nor blasphemers of their goddess. He gave a passing rebuke to Demetrius and the members of his guild, telling them that if they had any grievance against any one, there was a proper procedure for them to follow. There were courts, and there were pro-consuls ; they could go before them. He finished by reminding them that their unruly proceedings were likely to recoil on their own heads. Then he dismissed the assembly.

By ones, twos, and threes, the people went shamefacedly out of the theatre, leaving the brethren unharmed ; but the riot put an end to Paul's work in Ephesus. Before he left the city he summoned some of the disciples to his lodgings, and spoke to them in words of exhortation ; then he departed for Greece. His stay in Ephesus had been marked by much activity, and much suffering. He speaks of himself as " dying daily ", of " fighting with wild beasts " there. Whether the latter expression is intended to be understood literally or figuratively, it indicates a period of suffering and trial, of which very little is recorded in the Acts of the Apostles.

CHAPTER XV

A LETTER TO CORINTH

DURING the time Paul was at Ephesus he wrote a letter to the Church at Corinth. It was a stern letter, full of rebuke ; but it has to be numbered with the lost letters of the Apostle. Later, certain persons, including some of the household of one Chloe, made him acquainted with the unsatisfactory state of affairs which existed in the Corinthian Church. The meeting was divided ; faction and strife were rife, and there was quarrelling among its members ; and evil practices were permitted to go on unrebuked. About the same time some of the members of the Church wrote to Paul submitting certain questions about various matters of faith and practice. The report, and the letter, made it necessary for Paul to write to them again ; the result is the letter which we know as the First Epistle to the Corinthians. It was written before Paul left Ephesus.

While no detailed account of Paul's letters can be given here, it is desirable that something should be said about them, for they give a real insight into the mind of the man, and illustrate what was happening among the Christians of the First Century.

The Epistle opens with a salutation to its readers. " Grace to you, and peace from God our Father and the Lord Jesus Christ." Such salutations are found in all Paul's letters, and this early one is a good illustration of others. The combination of terms, grace and peace, is characteristic of Christianity. Grace means favour and kindliness ; peace is elsewhere defined as the " peace of God that passeth all understanding". Together they constitute a great ideal for Christians, but it was an ideal to which those in Corinth had not yet risen.

Paul soon got to the reason for the letter, for he exhorted them all to speak the same things, and end the feuds that existed among them. In their divisions they bandied about the names of Paul and Cephas, Apollos and Christ, using them as party labels. The name of Christ seems to be a strange one to adopt for a particular party in the Church ; Christ was Master and Lord of all its members. It seems as if it was adopted by a strongly Jewish section which contended that Christ complied with the provisions of the Mosaic Law, and that Christians should do the same to whatever nation they may belong. They probably thought that Cephas (Peter) had compromised their position by his actions in preaching to Cornelius.

Rebuking this spirit of rivalry among them Paul reminded them of the circumstances under which he first visited Corinth, telling them that he came with a firm determination not to know anything among them but Jesus Christ and him crucified. They had received that message, and they must stand to it. Paul and Apollos had both built on that foundation, and the building they had helped to erect was a temple in which God might dwell. Schism and schismatics could have no place in such a building.

Paul's treatment of the divided state of the Church furnishes a remarkable insight into his character. He said, " Who then is Apollos ? and what is Paul ? (Note how he names Apollos before himself.) Ministers through whom ye believed, and each as the Lord gave to him. I planted, Apollos watered, but God gave the increase. So then neither is he that planteth anything, neither he that watereth, but God that giveth the increase ". The true gentlemanly character of the man comes out in passages like these.

An appreciation of the principles of Christianity leads to an avoidance of evil and to the manifestation of holiness and personal purity. It was necessary to emphasize these points in a city like Corinth where the morals of the public were exceedingly low. In the epistle mention is made of a number of the vilest forms of sin, with the comment, " and such were some of you ". No wonder that it was necessary to say to people with such a past, " Purge out the old leaven, that ye may be a new lump, even as ye are unleavened. For our Passover also hath been sacrificed, even Christ. Wherefore let us keep the feast, not with old leaven, neither with the leaven of malice and wickedness ; but with the unleavened bread of sincerity and truth ".

A knowledge of the low moral condition of the people of Corinth prepares the reader for some of the matters dealt with in the letter. A large portion of it is taken up with the reports that had reached Paul. There was gross immorality in the Church ; personal feelings ran so high that brethren instituted law-suits against one another. It was certainly a deplorable state of affairs, and not much would be gained by enlarging on this aspect of the conduct of the believers. It will be quite sufficient if the early portion of the letter is read.

The central part of the letter is introduced by the words, "Now concerning the things whereof ye wrote ". Like all young communities the members of the Church in Corinth had come up against various difficulties. What were they to do in such and such a case ? There were questions concerning marriage, and of eating food that had been sacrificed to idols. The answers given to these questions can be read in the epistle. There is, however, a self-revealing passage in connection with the latter question that must be commented on, for it illustrates the mind of Paul as it bore on his own conduct as it affected others. He was ready to give up anything if persistence in it would prejudice the welfare of another. " Wherefore ", he says, " if meat cause my brother to stumble I will eat no flesh for evermore, that I make not my brother to stumble." Such a saying shows that Paul was the kind of man suited to be a leader of men.

Passing over much that invites comment, questions concerning the meetings for the Breaking of Bread, matters of fellowship, and so forth, two long chapters deal with what are called " spiritual gifts ". All these must be passed over, though it may be wondered why Paul should have troubled to deal with such a question as the necessity for a woman to have her head covered when in the Church.

The reason for the emphasis laid upon the matter will be seen when it is known that in Corinth only one type of woman, and that the worst, talked in public and appeared without a veil. Remember the words quoted some time back—" and such were some of you ! " Now that they had forsaken their old ways it was necessary for them to avoid anything that might seem to imply that some of " the old leaven " was left. It was essential that they should act in such a way that the public would not be led to suppose they were in any way akin to the class who acted in such a fashion.

Although the two chapters on spiritual gifts may seem to be comparatively unimportant today, there suddenly appears one of the really important illustrations of the relationships of the body of Christians. Paul likens the various members of the Church to the various parts of the human body, thereby illustrating the essential unity that should characterize the members of the Church of Christ. Individuals may be legs or arms, eyes or ears ; their abilities may be as different as the functions of those parts of the body are, yet they all constitute one body. The idea is so simple and yet so profound. It takes us back to the early chapter where Paul asked the pointed question, " Is Christ divided ? "

In between the two chapters which deal with spiritual gifts, Paul suddenly breaks into the continuity of his instructions, and introduces one of the most charming chapters in all his writings. It is worth reproducing at length.

If I speak with the tongues of men and of angels, but have not love, I have become sounding brass or a clanging cymbal. And if I have the gift of prophecy, and know all mysteries and all knowledge ; and if I have all faith, so as to remove mountains, but have not love, I am nothing. And if I bestow all my goods to feed the poor, and if I give my body to be burned, but have not love, it profiteth me nothing.

Love has patience and is kind ;
Love envieth not ;
Love is not vainglorious,
Is not puffed up,
Acts not unseemly,
Seeketh not its own,
Is not quickly provoked,
Taketh not account of evil ;
Rejoiceth not in unrighteousness,
But rejoiceth with the Truth ;

Beareth all things,
Believeth all things,
Hopeth all things,
Endureth all things.

Love never faileth ;
But whether there be prophecies, they shall
    be done away,
Whether there be tongues they shall cease ;
Whether there be knowledge it shall be
    done away.

For we know in part, and we prophesy in
    part ;
But when that which is perfect is come
That which is in part shall be done away.

When I was a child I spake as a child,
I felt as a child ;
I reasoned as a child ;
Now that I am become a man
I have put away childish things.

For now we see in a mirror, darkly ;
But then face to face.
Now I know in part ;
But then shall I know even as also I have
    been known.

But now abideth faith, hope, love, these
    three ;
And the greatest of these is love.

The word " love " is used with a great variety of meanings today ; people often use it for things they merely like. The Greeks had three words for love, whereas we use one for them all, making it apply to such different manifestations as the love of parents for their children, of husbands for wives, or a fondness for some flower or sweetmeat. When love is mentioned in the New Testament, remember that in the majority of cases, it means a love such as is defined in Paul's great hymn to love. It is the love of God, Who so loved the world that He gave His only begotten Son, that whosoever believeth on him may obtain everlasting life. It is the love that Jesus had in view when he said, " Greater love hath no man than this, that a man lay down his life for his friends ". These illustrate love toward the human race, and show what is meant when reference is made to the love men should have for God and Christ.

When Paul had finished dealing with spiritual gifts he passed to the question of the resurrection of the body. The reader is recommended to read this chapter (the fifteenth) carefully, and to think about it. It finishes with a song of praise about victory over death, and an exhortation to be stedfast, immovable, always abounding in the work of the Lord.

Then, having sung the praises of love, and having raised the thoughts of his readers to the contemplation of victory over death and the grave, he suddenly turns to practical instructions about the collections that were being made for the help of others ! " Now concerning the collection ", he says !

Paul concluded the letter with a personal addition. " The salutation of me Paul with mine own hand. If any man loveth not the Lord, let him be anathema. Maran atha. The grace of the Lord Jesus Christ be with you. My love be with you all in Christ Jesus. Amen."

If the epistle is read through, still more if it is studied, it will be realized that Paul was a versatile man, and that it was a great thing for the early Christians to have such a man among them. Such men often have enemies, and when the Second Epistle comes under notice it will be seen that Paul had some. He was too forthright for some in his days ; too definitely committed to the cause of Christ, to go through life without making enemies.

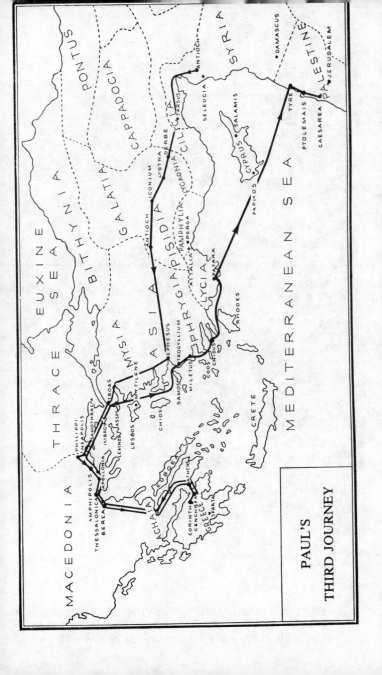

PAUL'S

THIRD JOURNEY

PAPYRUS MANUSCRIPT SHOWING SECTION OF PAUL'S EPISTLES IN GREEK (Gal. 6:10—Phil. 1:1)
Chester Beatty II ms. Early 3rd Century. Original size 8½" × 6"

CHAPTER XVI

MORE LETTERS ;
RETURNING TO JERUSALEM

WHEN Paul left Ephesus he took passage in a coasting vessel as far as Troas, where "a door" had been opened for him. It had been first opened during his stay in Ephesus, when "all that dwelt in Asia" heard the word of the Lord. Though there was much to be done, and plenty to occupy his thoughts, Paul was anxious, for he had hoped to find Titus there with news from Corinth, and Titus had not arrived. He says of himself, "I had no rest for my spirit because I found not Titus my brother". He was depressed too by the events that had caused him to leave Ephesus ; he was "weighed down exceedingly", despairing even of life, for he had "sentence of death within himself". Great men are much moved by such feelings at times, but they show their greatness by facing their difficulties and not permitting themselves to be overcome by them. That is what Paul did ; he looked at the depressing circumstances, and saw that the reason for his troubles was that he should not have trust in himself, but in God who raiseth the dead.

Paul soon left Troas for Macedonia and Greece. His object was not so much to preach

the gospel as to confirm believers in the faith ;
he therefore gave "much exhortation", urging
them to abide stedfastly in the love and labour
of the Truth.

His one great anxiety was to know the effect
of the letter he had sent to the Corinthians.
That was why he longed for the return of Titus.
Speaking of himself at this time he says, " For
even when we were come into Macedonia, our
flesh had no ease, but we were afflicted on every
side ; without were fightings, within were fears ".
Then at last Titus arrived bringing news of
affairs in Corinth, and Paul was able to say,
" Nevertheless he that comforteth the lowly, even
God, comforted us by the coming of Titus ".

Though the news Titus brought was not
altogether satisfactory it was sufficiently so to
bring cheer to Paul. He told of the repentance
that had been shown on account of the sins that
had been rebuked ; of the zeal of the brethren for
Paul. Titus had been impressed by the sincerity
of the believers in their mourning over the past ;
so Paul was comforted, and " exceedingly joyed
the more for the joy of Titus ".

The allusions just made are found in the
second letter Paul wrote to Corinth, which
must be noted, though no attempt will be made
to deal with it in detail.

The rebukes contained in the previous letter
had caused a reformation in the ecclesia, and the
further letter was intended to give them comfort.
The preamble breathes this idea, for in it Paul

refers to God as " the Father of mercies and the God of all comfort " Who had comforted Paul so that he in turn might comfort others.

An important feature of the letter is Paul's assertion of his apostolic authority which had been impugned by a section of believers who were opposed to him, that is, the Judaizing party which still persisted in their efforts to bring Christians under bondage to the Jewish Law. In dealing with this matter Paul, as it were, justified himself against those who traduced him, by giving a list of his experiences. In the previous chapters enough has been recorded to make him stand out as one of the greatest characters referred to in the Bible. Yet what has been mentioned includes only a fraction of what he actually endured. His summary of his past life in the service of the gospel may be read in the Foreword, and there is no need to repeat it here. If it is read through it will be seen that it involved incessant labour, sufferings, weariness, and anxiety, as well as the patient endurance of a " thorn in the flesh ", the " messenger of Satan " to buffet him, and all borne for the sake of Christ and those who were Christ's. He took no credit for himself, all the glory he ascribed to God : " Yet not I, but the grace of God which was given me ".

In addition to the Foreword one other passage from this letter may be quoted as it indicates some of his experiences at the time : " We are pressed on every side yet not straightened, perplexed yet not in despair, persecuted yet not forsaken, smitten down yet not destroyed ; always bearing about in the body the dying of Jesus that the life also of Jesus may be manifested in our body ".

In this letter he makes another reference to the collection that was being made for the poor in Jerusalem. With gentle urgency he wrote, " As touching the ministering to the saints it is superfluous for me to write unto you ". The very wording of the passage is an indication of the gentleman in Paul. It is tactful and kindly, yet it is urgent. " I thought it necessary therefore to intreat the brethren that they would go before unto you and make up beforehand your promised bounty ". And the reason for this kindly urgency was, as Paul wrote : " lest we (that we say not ye) should be put to shame ".

The closing expressions of the epistle are worthy of repetition. As in other cases, the words were probably written by Paul himself. " Finally, brethren, farewell. Be perfected ; be comforted ; be of the same mind ; live in peace ; and the God of love and peace shall be with you . . . The grace of our Lord Jesus Christ, and the love of God, and the communion of the Holy Spirit, be with you all. " It is a prayer that anyone would be glad to think was being offered for him.

With the departure of Titus to Corinth with this letter, Paul was left in Macedonia.

For some months he continued there, then he left, and made his way to Greece. His intention was to go to Corinth, and sail from thence to Palestine, so that he might arrive in Jerusalem in time for Pentecost.

There was in Corinth at the time a large gathering of representative Christians. Paul was accompanied by those who represented the Ephesian Christians, and some from Derbe. Several Macedonians were there. They had assembled to take part in carrying to Jerusalem the alms that had been provided by the Gentile Christians for the benefit of the poor in Jerusalem.

The original intention was to leave Corinth together, but at the last moment the plan was altered. News reached the Christians of Corinth that a plot had been made to get rid of Paul. The plot was a simple one. It was known that the party were to travel by one of the pilgrim ships that carried the Jews of Greece to Judea to keep the approaching festival. Some of the fanatical element purposed to seize Paul at a favourable moment, probably by night, and drop him into the sea.

The discovery of the plot caused Paul to alter his plans, so he arranged to travel by land to another port. Among those who were to have travelled with him were Sopater the son of Pyrrhus of Berea, Aristarchus and Secundus of Macedonia, Gaius of Derbe, Tychicus and Trophimus of Asia, and his son in the faith Timothy. Luke, too, was with the company, for the record again introduces the pronoun " us ". Owing to the change in plans it was decided that these should go by ship as arranged and meet Paul at Troas.

The record in the Acts of the Apostles gives no reason for so many representatives of various Churches going to Jerusalem at this time. As stated above they were going with the " bounty " collected by the Gentile Churches. Paul himself gives an indication of this in his address before Felix. He said, " I came to bring alms to my nation, and offerings ". The gathering of these Gentile Christians was necessary ; they were not only to carry the bounty to Jerusalem, but were to supervise the dispensing of it. In a letter written about this time, that to the Romans, Paul says, " Now I go unto Jerusalem, ministering to the saints. For it hath pleased them of Macedonia and Achaia to make a certain contribution for the poor among the saints that are in Jerusalem ". It was a gracious movement on the part of the Churches among the Gentiles, showing their goodwill towards the members of the Church in Jerusalem.

Just before the journey commenced Paul heard that Phoebe, a Christian of Cenchrea (the port of Corinth), was about to visit Rome. It gave him an opportunity to send a letter to the Christians of that city, whom he had long desired to meet.

The Epistle to the Romans occupies such an important position among the Christian writings that it is necessary to give some attention to it. Paul was a man of vision, and he saw in the Empire of Rome something of what he hoped to see organized in the Christian Church. Rome, or rather its rulers, regarded the city and the Empire as one great organization, and Paul's idea was that the Christian community should be one and indivisible. If such an idea was to become an accomplished fact it was desirable that there should be a strong and united Church in the Capital. At that time there was nothing of the kind ; the Christians of Rome met in private houses ; hence the allusions to " the Church that is in their house ", after the mention of certain names towards the end of the letter. History has shown that such a thing was not to be, at any rate so far as the true Church was concerned. Yet the idea was a great one, and the letter to the Romans was connected with that idea. It must be remembered that the letter was written before the Empire had begun to persecute the Church.

As the letter was not written to solve local problems, or to settle local difficulties, there is less of the personality of the writer than in the majority of Paul's letters ; indeed, it is more like a treatise setting forth the principles of the Christian faith. It is for this reason that it is supremely valuable. This point is emphasized in the first and last chapters, in both of which reference is made to " the obedience of faith ". The epistle falls naturally into sections, and in any attempt to give a brief account of its teaching, it is necessary to keep the sections separate.

Two points dealt with in the opening section call for notice ; first Paul's earnest desire to go to Rome. He remembered the Christians of the city, whom he had never seen, unceasingly in his prayers, beseeching that " *by any means* (a most interesting expression when the way in which it was answered is seen) now at length I may be prospered by the will of God to come unto you. For I long to see you, that I may impart unto you some spiritual gift ; that I with you may be comforted ". Paul little thought as he dictated these words that he was just entering on a course that was to bring him to Rome.

The second point is Paul's description of the Roman world of his day. There is, surely, no more dreadful passage of literature than that contained in the first chapter of this epistle. It need not be repeated here, but it may be pointed out that contemporary evidence fully supports the various statements that are made concerning the depravity of the times, as exhibited in Roman society.

Some space is given up to the mutual suspicions of Jews and Gentiles. The tendencies that had been manifested in Galatia were incipient among the Christians in Rome. If there is no fear of such tendencies affecting Christians of today, it may be attributed to a very large extent, to Paul's comments, and to his question and answer. " What advantage then

hath the Jew ? or what is the profit of circumcision ? Much every way ; first of all that they
were intrusted with the oracles of God ". Could
anything more be said to commend the Scriptures
of the Old Testament to Christians of today ?

The great theme of the earlier part of the
Epistle is that of justification by faith—not by
faith alone, as some have said, but by a faith
that works by love. This most important section
of the epistle occupies chapters five to eight.
Comment is out of the question, and every reader
should read the section through at one sitting.
Its argument is that sin entered into the world by
Adam's transgression, and that by sin came
death. The antidote to this is in Jesus Christ,
who provides life for those who come to him
in the appointed way. Life is in Christ ; the
appointed way is indicated in the statement,
" Buried therefore with him through baptism
into death . . . if we have become united with
him by the likeness of his death, we shall be
also by the likeness of his resurrection . . . If
we died with Christ, we believe that we shall also
live with him ".

An important part of this section of the
epistle is autobiographical. It is found in the
seventh chapter. " I was alive apart from the
Law once, but when the commandment came,
sin revived and I died." " Sin beguiled me,
and by it slew me." " That which I do I know
not, for not that I would, that do I practise, but
what I hate, that I do." There is an interesting

variation of this passage as given in *The Englishman's Greek New Testament*. It reads, " For what I work out I do not own ; for not what I will, this I do ; but what I hate, this I practise". If ever a man had tried to do what he could to keep the Law of his God, it was Paul ! Yet that is how he sums up his past life. The greatest Christian of the age, he had to write, " I know that in me, that is in my flesh, dwelleth no good thing, for to will is present with me, but to do that which is good is not ". If that were all that was to be said, the best of us might feel hopeless. Paul was not hopeless, for, asking, as if in despair, " Who shall deliver me out of the body of this death ? " he answers in a triumphant burst of confidence, " I thank God through Jesus Christ our Lord ! "

With such an assurance it is no wonder that Paul closed this section of the epistle with a doxology. " In all these things we are more than conquerors through him that loved us. For I am persuaded that neither death, nor life, nor angels, nor principalities, nor things present, nor things to come, nor powers, nor height, nor depth, nor any other creature, shall be able to separate us from the love of God, which is in Christ Jesus our Lord ".

The next section might have for its title " Israel's Place in the Plan ". Together with the previous section there is here summed up the things concerning the Kingdom of God and of the Name of the Lord Jesus Christ. Again all that can be said here is, read the section (chapters nine to eleven) ; It should be read through at one sitting if it is desired to appreciate it at its true worth. Seeing all that is comprehended in these three chapters, it is not surprising to find that they end with another doxology.

> " O the depths of the riches,
>> Both of the wisdom and the knowledge of God !
> How unsearchable are his judgments,
> And his ways past tracing out !
> For who hath known the mind of the Lord?
> Or who hath been his counsellor ?
> Or who hath first given to him,
>> And it shall be recompensed unto him again ?
> For OF HIM, and THROUGH HIM, UNTO HIM are all things.
> To him be the glory for ever. Amen."

After this there are admonitions and exhortations, introduced by the words, " I beseech you therefore, brethren, by the mercies of God "—the mercies which have been set out in all their beauty in the previous sections of the epistle. Finally, after a long list of salutations, he ends with one more doxology. " Now to him that is able to stablish you according to my gospel, and the preaching of Jesus Christ, according to the revelation of the mystery which hath been kept in silence through times eternal, but now is manifested, and by the Scriptures of the prophets, according to the commandment of the Eternal God, is made known unto all the nations unto obedience of faith ; to the only Wise God, through Jesus Christ, to whom be the glory for ever. Amen ".

This last doxology was evidently written by Paul himself, for a little before we read " I, Tertius, who write the epistle, salute you in the Lord ". Then Paul took up his pen and finished the letter with these words.

After despatching the letter Paul made his way toward Jerusalem. Accompanied by Luke he journeyed to Troas, where the rest of the party joined him.

In the account of the events that took place at Troas an interesting light is thrown on the practices of the believers of those days. On the first day of the week, Luke tells us, they were gathered together to break bread. This is the first time this ordinance is mentioned in connection with the first day of the week, but it is mentioned in such a way as to suggest that it was already a usual custom. The rite is a wise institution, reminding those who participate in it of their association with " the body and blood of the Lord ".

On this occasion the word of exhortation, usual at such meetings, was spoken by Paul. It was nothing of the " bright, brief, and brotherly " character common among some at the present day. How long Paul spoke is not known, but, whatever the time may have been when he commenced to speak, he continued until midnight ! Of course the occasion was an unusual one, for Paul was to leave the next day.

Picture the scene. In an upper room, perhaps in an obscure quarter of the town, the disciples had come together for the double purpose of taking part in the usual service for the Breaking of Bread, and to say farewell to a dearly beloved brother. The room was crowded ; at least one of those who were present was sitting in the window. It was night, and many lamps were in the room. As the meeting continued the atmosphere became closer and closer, and nothing but the intense interest, and the emotion, of the occasion, enabled those in the room to resist the influence of the heavy air. The young man sitting in the window could not do so. Drowsiness stole over him ; his eyes closed, his head nodded, and he slept. Still the address continued until suddenly, to the consternation of all, he overbalanced and fell from the window to the street, three stories below. There he lay, dead. The author of the narrative, Luke, was a doctor, and his statement may be taken as a definite indication that it was not a case of mere unconsciousness, but of actual death.

The effect on those who were in the room may be imagined. The meeting broke up. Paul ran down the stairs, embraced the young man, saying, " Make ye no ado ; for his life is in him ". After all the excitement caused by this event the meeting was resumed, and the ceremony of

Breaking Bread took place. A meal followed, after which Paul resumed speaking, and spoke through the hours of darkness, until the first streaks of daylight in the eastern sky marked the break of another day. Then they went with him to the ship.

CHAPTER XVII

A FAREWELL CHARGE

From Troas Paul resumed his way toward Jerusalem. The main body of the party took ship from Troas, but Paul stayed in the town for a short time. As the ship had to sail round Cape Lectum, and call at Assos, it would take a longer time than was required to walk from Troas to Assos. Paul evidently desired to stay with the brethren of Troas as long as he could ; it gave him a little time longer with them, especially if some of them accompanied him on his walk between the two places.

When Paul joined the party at Assos the completed company sailed on, passing Mitelene, Samos, and other places, and then called at Miletus. Here the ship was to unload a part of the cargo, and to take in more. The two operations would take a sufficiently long time for a message to be sent to the brethren at Ephesus. A member of Paul's party went as fast as he could by sea and land to Ephesus, and representatives of the Church there made their way with Paul's messenger to Miletus.

The meeting with the Ephesian elders was a moving one, and the address Paul gave was serious and sobering. Paul commenced by reminding them of the time he had spent among them, " serving the Lord with all humility and many tears ". He referred to the plots that had been made against him by the Jews, and how he had not shrunk from declaring unto them anything that was profitable ; and how he had taught them, publicly and from house to house. The subject of his teaching is defined as " repentance toward God and faith toward the Lord Jesus Christ ".

The allusions are interesting ; they show how little we know of the details of his life. There were "plots " against him in Ephesus, but in the account given in the Acts of the Apostles there is no mention of any plots made by the Jews of Ephesus ; the only thing of the kind mentioned is the riot in the theatre, which was engineered by the silversmith. Demetrius and his trade guild.

After this brief retrospect Paul turned to the future. He spoke of the visit to Jerusalem which he had in mind, and told how, wherever he went, the Holy Spirit made known that bonds and afflictions awaited him. " But ", he said, " I hold not my life of any account as dear unto myself, so that I may finish my course with joy, and the ministry which I received from the Lord Jesus, to testify the gospel of the grace of God ". These were great words from a noble man. From some lips they might savour of self-advertisement ; coming from one who had already passed through such experiences as are referred to in the Foreword, there is no such spirit in them. The whole life of Paul belies such an idea, and there was nothing in the words beyond that which his whole life showed to be characteristic of him.

For himself such things mattered little ; his concern was about his hearers, and those to whom they ministered. He knew that apostasy and trouble would arise, and with forebodings concerning such tendencies he went on to say, " And now, behold, I know that ye all, among whom I went about preaching the Kingdom, shall see my face no more. Wherefore I testify to you this day that I am pure from the blood of all men, for I shrank not from declaring unto you the whole counsel of God. Take heed unto yourselves, and to all the flock, in which the Holy Spirit hath made you overseers, to feed the Church of God which He purchased with His own blood. For I know that after my departing grievous wolves shall enter in among you, not sparing the flock ; and from among your own selves shall men arise, speaking perverse things, to draw away the disciples after them ".

The words must have fallen on the ears of the listeners like the strokes of a hammer. " From among your own selves ! " " Grievous wolves ! " One can imagine them exclaiming " God forbid ! " Yet the words were true, and it was not long before the worst forebodings of Paul were realized. Only six years later Paul wrote, " This thou knowest that all that are in Asia (and Ephesus was the capital of that province) turned away from me ". In these days temptations may come in different ways; open persecution, involving striving unto blood, has not been among the evils of the times; yet trials will come and all must be on their guard.

Words of warning followed. "Therefore, watch ye, remembering that by the space of three years I ceased not to admonish every one night and day with tears. And now I commend you to God, and to the word of his grace, which is able to build you up, and to give you the inheritance among all them that are sanctified." Better advice could not be given, then or now. The word of God's grace is an inexhaustible store from which wisdom and strength may be gained to combat the perilous influences of the times.

It is rather popular to underrate the Bible. Circulating by millions it has, in a sense, become common. When a wagon load of hay was paid for a portion of a Bible, the book was valued. This is not the place to "preach", though it is always a time to give a word of advice. The advice is very simple. "Don't be influenced by modern neglect of the Bible; read it; read it regularly and consistently, and think about what you read."

In concluding his address Paul once more referred to his manner of life among them. " I coveted no man's silver, or gold, or apparel ", he said; pointing out that he had ministered to his own necessities and to the needs of those who had been with him, thus setting an example, and showing how that so labouring they " ought to help the weak, and to remember the words of the Lord Jesus, who himself said, ' It is more blessed to give than to receive ' ".

The words are not found in the gospels, but they were among the words of Jesus that were treasured in those days. None of our gospels had been written then, but collections of the Master's sayings were treasured by the Christians of the time.

Paul had finished. Silence and sadness followed his words. Then Paul suggested that they should pray ; pray that God would guide and protect them in the coming days. Picture the scene : a little circle of sorrowing disciples and, in their midst, a kneeling figure—the teacher whom, as yet, at all events, they revered. He prayed that God's blessing might rest upon those present, and the many in Ephesus to whom they were to minister. We do not know the words he uttered, but can imagine their theme. Then came the parting. They all wept, fell on Paul's neck and ardently kissed him. Had he not said that they should see his face no more ?

Many times the members of that little company must have dwelt upon that sorrowful and solemn parting. The warning, the advice, and the prayer, must have remained vividly in their minds. And yet, as has been said already, Paul had to write, " All that are in Asia turned away from me ". Was his prayer in vain ? Did his labour in Ephesus result in nothing? By no means. The defection of the Asian brethren was a passing phase. Thirty years later Christ was able to say of the Church in Ephesus, " I know thy works, and thy toil, and patience, and that thou canst not bear evil men ; and didst try them which call themselves apostles, and are not, and didst find them false, and thou hast patience, and didst bear for my name's sake, and hast not grown weary ".

The meeting was over ; its emotional stress is shown by a word Luke uses in recording the incident ; we " dragged " ourselves away from them. Then Paul and his company continued on their way to Jerusalem.

With favourable winds their progress was rapid. They soon reached Cos ; next day they were at Rhodes ; whence they sailed to Patara, a town on the Asian mainland, where they left the ship. There they found one going to Tyre. Christianity had been established a long time in that city, and there they stayed seven days. There was no need for hurry now ; there was ample time to get to Jerusalem for Pentecost.

At Tyre the Spirit revealed to some of the disciples of the town what would result from Paul's visit to Jerusalem. They endeavoured to persuade him to give up the journey, but without avail. A purpose was being worked out, all unrealized at the time, the outcome of which was to be an answer to his earnest desire, expressed in his own phrase, " After that, I must see Rome ".

After the seven days Paul and his party, accompanied by the Christians of Tyre, with their children, went to the seashore to find the ship that was to take him to Caesarea. There was another little meeting on the beach, where prayer was offered up before they bade each other farewell. The ship on which they sailed called at Ptolemais, where the brethren of that place visited them. Next day they travelled by sea to Caesarea, where they stayed in the house of Philip, who had been one of the " deacons " appointed in the early days of the Church.

Here another intimation was given of the danger that awaited Paul at the end of the journey. Agabus, a prophet of whom we have heard before, took hold of the girdle of Paul's mantle, loosened it, and bound his own hands and feet with it, saying, " Thus saith the Holy Spirit, So shall the Jews at Jerusalem bind the man that owneth this girdle, and shall deliver him into the hands of the Gentiles ". The prediction, illustrated in this dramatic fashion, had a powerful effect upon all who were present. Not only those of Caesarea, but those who had heard him say before, " I hold not my life of any account, as dear unto myself", gave way to grief, and besought him to desist from his purpose. It was useless. Paul's mind was set on the object of his journey. He had been entrusted with the gift of the Gentile Churches to the poor of Jerusalem, and he was going to see it through. His answer was, " What do ye, weeping and breaking my heart? For I am ready not to be bound only, but also to die at Jerusalem for the name of the Lord Jesus ". It was the only answer that could have been expected from him, and they desisted, saying, " The will of the Lord be done ".

It was not that Paul underrated the dangers that threatened him. As has been seen, he asked for the prayers of the Christians of Rome that he might be delivered from unbelievers in Judea, and that the offerings he was carrying to the city might be accepted by the saints there. He expected trouble, not only from the unbelieving Jews of Jerusalem, but, may be, from some of those who were numbered as Christians there.

From Caesarea to Jerusalem is but a short journey, and Paul and his companions were soon welcomed by the brethren of the city. The reception must have relieved his mind from one of the forebodings that impressed him when he wrote his letter to the Christians of Rome.

CHAPTER XVIII

IN JERUSALEM

WHEN Paul and his fellow travellers reached
Jerusalem arrangements were made for them to
hand over the bounty they had brought from the
Gentile Churches. Timothy, half a Jew, represented the donors of Galatia ; Aristarchus and
Secundus acted for Philippi ; Tychicus and
Trophimus represented the Ephesians and the
members of various churches in Asia ; in addition
there was Sopater of Berea. The handing over
was, no doubt, done as part of a ceremony ;
it was a graceful act on the part of the Churches
of the various districts, for by it they proclaimed
their unity in the gospel with the Church in
Jerusalem and its members. For a short time they
were able to show their rejoicing in the " unity
of the Spirit ".

Since the days when Paul first visited
Jerusalem as a Christian, the Church in the city
had grown. It had then been a persecuted
body ; by the time of this fraternal meeting the
persecution had died down, and James was able
to speak of tens of thousands (Gk. myriads) of
Jews who believed. In the main, at all events,
they still conformed to the requirements of the
Mosaic Law in many ways.

The leaders of the Church were faced with a
difficult problem. Paul was the leader of that

section of the Christian body that realized the freedom that belief in Christ gave from the bondage of the Mosaic Law. That was the basis of the charge that was soon made against him, and though, as is usually the case, many of the things they said were either untrue, or greatly exaggerated, there was sufficient truth in what they said to stir up those who were still zealous for the Law.

With a view to modifying these feelings it was suggested that Paul should, in a semi-public way, show that the charges were unfounded. " Thou seest, brother ", the Christians of the Capital said, " how many myriads there are among the Jews of them which have believed, and they are all zealous for the Law." In the circumstances it was suggested that Paul should undertake to defray the expenses of certain men who were under a vow. There was no suggestion that he should in any way compromise the principles for which he had striven so ardently on behalf of the Gentile Christians. Of course, the proposed action was something of a compromise, but it had the merit, so the leaders of the Church thought, of proving to Jewish Christians that Paul was " a son of the Law ". Paul agreed to the suggestion, and on the very next day he and four men went into the temple to commence the ritual associated with vows.

The ceremony involved attendance in a room in the temple area for seven days, and these were almost finished when the events which the Spirit

had foretold took place. It was the time of
Pentecost, and there were Jews in the city from
all parts of the Empire, including Asia. Some
of these had seen Paul in the city with an
Ephesian named Trophimus. Now they saw Paul
beyond the " middle wall of partition ", which
marked the boundary beyond which no Gentile
was allowed to go. It was an opportunity such
as they could hardly have hoped for, and they
took immediate advantage of it. They called
to the Jews in the Temple, " Men, Israelites,
help ! This is the man that teacheth all men
everywhere against the people, and the Law,
and this place ; and moreover he brought
Greeks into the Temple, and hath defiled this
holy place ". It was a lie, but it served their
purpose. No charge could have stirred the Jews
more effectually. A great crowd assembled at
once, some of whom laid hands on Paul, and
dragged him out of the Temple.

Had the Jews been left alone Paul would
certainly have been killed on the spot. They
were, however, a subject race, even though they
did not like to admit it, and they were not
allowed to forget the fact. At the north-western
corner of the Temple was the Tower of Antonia,
and with it was a parade ground where the
Roman garrison carried on its exercises. A set
of stairs led from the Castle to the roof of the
cloisters, and another from the roof to the Temple
courts. Because of the excitable character of the
Jews, especially at festival times, a garrison was

kept, strong enough to cope with any untoward event that might take place. A watch was kept from the tower, so that immediate notice could be given of any threatening occurrence. Such a notice was now given, and the Captain in charge, Claudius Lysias, was told that the whole place was in an uproar.

Claudius acted promptly, and, accompanied by centurions and soldiers, made his way to where the uproar was worst. The appearance of the soldiers caused the mob to cease beating Paul, and the chief captain took charge of the situation.

He now took hold of Paul, and gave instruction that he should be put in chains. His action was quite understandable, for the violence of the multitude suggested that Paul must have been guilty of some unusual crime. He tried to find out what was wrong, who Paul was, and what he had been doing. It was impossible to obtain any reasonable answer from the crowd, for some said one thing and some another. He then gave instructions that Paul should be taken into the castle.

As the soldiers obeyed this command the violence of the crowd was so great that they not only had to guard Paul, but the two to whom he was chained had to carry him until, amid shouts of "Away with him", they reached the stairs. There he was set down, and there Claudius Lysias had his first shock. Paul addressed him in Greek, and requested to be allowed to speak to the people. Claudius had come to the conclusion that the man he had rescued was an Egyptian who had caused considerable trouble a short time before. He had told his followers that the walls of Jerusalem would fall at his command, and had led them to the Mount of Olives to witness the event. The crowd had been dispersed and some hundreds of his followers had been slain, but the Egyptian had escaped.

" Dost thou know Greek ? " Claudius asked. " Art not thou the Egyptian who before these days caused a confusion, and led out into the wilderness four thousand men that were assassins ? "

" No ", Paul answered with a dignity that must have further surprised Claudius, " I am a Jew of Tarsus, in Cilicia, a citizen of no insignificant city."

It gave Claudius rather more respect for the man before him. Then Paul further said, " I beseech thee, give me leave to speak unto the people."

The leave was given, and standing there upon the stairs, Paul, bruised and bound, with his clothing torn, beckoned with his hand, a characteristic action of his, and a sudden silence fell over the people. There must have been some strange power in Paul, that, standing there, facing his would-be murderers, such a gesture, or the sound of his voice that followed, should change a howling mob into a quiet assembly.

Amid a profound silence Paul spoke in the Hebrew language, a language which the Captain evidently did not know ; so that the words uttered conveyed no meaning to him. Paul told of his early life as a Jew of Tarsus ; of his coming to Jerusalem, where he was brought up at the feet of Gamaliel, who had instructed him according to the strict manner of the Law. He was then zealous for God, " as ", he said, " ye are all this day ". He told how he had persecuted the Christians, even unto death. He told them, too, that the High Priest could bear witness to these matters if he would, and so led on to the journey that had brought him face to face with the great crisis of his life.

In some detail he narrated the events that had taken place on the way to Damascus ; of the voice from heaven, of the blindness that had ensued, of his being led into Damascus, and of the visit of Ananias. Finally he referred to a vision he had in the very Temple by which he was now speaking, where he had heard the voice of Jesus of Nazareth saying, " Make haste and get thee quickly out of Jerusalem, because they will not receive of thee testimony concerning me ".

But he had urged, " Lord, they themselves know that I imprisoned and beat in every synagogue them that believed on thee, and when the blood of thy witness Stephen was shed, I also was standing by and consenting, and keeping the garments of them that slew him ".

It had seemed so natural to him, and he seems to have thought it would have convinced them. " They will listen to me ", had been his thought in the past ; they will realize that such a tremendous change would not take place in a man's life without some cause, equally tremendous ! So Paul continued, and told of the Lord's reply, " Depart, for I will send thee forth far hence unto the Gentiles ".

Up to this point his audience had listened amid a deep silence, but at the sound of that last hated word they were raised to a great frenzy, and a shout went up, " Away with such a fellow from the earth ". Their actions showed their feelings, and if Claudius could not understand the words he heard, he understood the actions he saw. The Jews threw off articles of clothing, cast handfuls of dust into the air, and pandemonium ensued. The captain could not understand this sudden outburst of rage. He thought the man upon the steps must be a criminal of the worst type to rouse such feelings. He took his prisoner into the castle and commanded the centurion, who was in attendance, to examine Paul by scourging.

It looked as if Paul would have to add another to his list of beatings, but this time he spoke before anything could be done.

" Is it lawful for you to scourge a man that is a Roman, and uncondemned ? " he asked the centurion.

The centurion at once stopped his preparations for the scourging, and went to the captain. He knew that it was a serious offence against Roman Law to scourge a Roman. " See, what art thou about to do ? " he said, " this man is a Roman."

It was the second shock Claudius Lysias had received. He went at once to where Paul was, and asked, " Art thou a Roman ? "

" Yes ", Paul answered.

Claudius Lysias was taken aback ; he had rendered himself liable to severe penalties in his haste to get at the facts. Yet it seemed hardly possible that the man before him, with clothes torn and bedraggled by the treatment he had received, should be a Roman citizen. He possessed the citizenship himself, but it had cost him a large sum of money, and he told Paul so, probably with an evidence of wonderment in his voice.

" But I was free born ! " Paul replied.

Claudius Lysias dared not ignore the answer ; he had already gone much further than he should, and he was no doubt aware that under Roman Law it was a very serious offence to claim the citizenship unless it was actually owned. The soldiers at once loosed the thongs with which they had bound Paul, and Paul was taken into the castle again.

Claudius Lysias lost no time in making further enquiries, for on the very next day he summoned the chief priests and the council to meet, and brought Paul before them.

What were Paul's thoughts as he stood before the Council that, some twenty-four years before, had condemned Stephen, a condemnation he himself had endorsed ? Did his mind picture the scene of the past ? It seems that he must have done so ; the very similarity of the surroundings would recall the previous occasion. Looking stedfastly at his accusers, Paul spoke in his defence, saying, " Brethren, I have lived before God in all good conscience until this day ".

The High Priest Ananias, who was president of the Sanhedrin, was a man notorious for his cruelty and injustice. With flagrant disregard of propriety and equity, he commanded that Paul should be smitten on the mouth. Paul was stung to reply, " God shall smite thee, thou whited wall : and sittest thou to judge me according to the Law, and commandest me to be smitten contrary to the Law ? "

It was a well merited rebuke, but some of those who stood there said, " Revilest thou God's High Priest ? " To them it was something like sacrilege ; they forgot that the essential thing in justice was to suit punishment to the crime, and to do so after proper enquiry had been made.

Paul at once disclaimed his knowledge that the speaker of the words was the High Priest, recognizing the obligation not to speak evil of the ruler of the people. His defective eyesight may have made it difficult to see who had given such an unpriestly instruction, or it may be, the words were uttered in the spirit of prophecy. In the wars that afterwards came upon the Jews the High Priest was compelled to flee ; his palace was burned over his head, and he had to hide himself. He was discovered by the Sicarii, who dragged him out and killed him.

It was clear to Paul that no justice was to be expected from the Council, and he adopted a course which, for the moment, gave him some respite. Raising his voice, he called out, " Men, brethren, I am a Pharisee, a son of Pharisees ; touching the hope and resurrection of the dead I am called in question ! "

The statement had the effect anticipated. the council was divided. The High Priest's party were Sadducees, and had no belief in the doctrine of a resurrection. Some of the members of the council were Pharisees, and they did believe in the resurrection. The two parties began wrangling between themselves ; a great discussion broke out, and feelings ran so high that, for a time, the Pharisees forgot their animosity against Paul, and defended their doctrine against Saddusaic unbelief. They even went so far as to suggest an angel, or a spirit, might have spoken to Paul ! The uproar became so great that the chief captain had to intervene, and take Paul back to the castle without having obtained any additional information about him.

If Paul was depressed by his experiences it was only what might have been expected, but during the night the Lord once more appeared to him with the message, " Be of good cheer, Paul ; for as thou hast testified concerning me at Jerusalem, so must thou bear witness at Rome ". That had now been his desire for some years, but he had never thought it would have been gratified by such means as these.

Another link in the chain of circumstances that was to take him to Rome then took place. Jewish spite, defrauded of its prey through the actions of Claudius Lysias, sought another way of obtaining its end. Some forty men bound themselves by an oath to refrain from all food and drink until they had assassinated Paul. They told the chief priests and elders of their purpose which evidently met with no objection on the part of these representatives of religion and justice. The dissension that had broken out in the council had evaporated ; hatred of Paul was deeper than the division between the two parties, and when the heat of the incident had passed off, they were again ready to join hands in opposing him.

By some means, Paul's nephew, now living in Jerusalem, became aware of the arrangements made for the assassination of his uncle, and went and told Paul. Paul referred him, to the chief captain. Claudius realized the gravity of the situation, and at once decided to remove Paul to Caesarea. An escort of 470 men, seventy of them mounted, was deemed necessary, a sufficient indication of the serious view that was taken of the matter. That they went from Jerusalem by night is a further proof that the danger was a real one. The foot soldiers accompanied the party as far as Antipatris, from which place Paul was taken on by the horsemen.

Caesarea was the headquarters of the Roman government ; the Procurator at the time was Felix. It was necessary to send some particulars of the circumstances that had made it desirable for the prisoner to be sent in this way, and it is interesting, and somewhat amusing, to see how Claudius Lysias made his own actions appear in the most favourable light, even though in doing so he somewhat misrepresented them. Here is his letter.

"Claudius Lysias unto the most excellent governor Felix, greeting. This man was seized by the Jews, and was about to be slain of them, when I came upon them with the soldiers, and rescued him, having learned that he was a Roman. And desiring to know the cause wherefore they accused him, I brought him down unto their council ; whom I found to be accused about questions of their Law, but to have nothing laid to his charge worthy of death or bonds. And when it was shown to me that there would be a plot against the man, I sent him to thee forthwith, charging his accusers also to speak against him before thee."

The incident leaves one wondering. The plotters were baulked of their prey. Did the forty men stand by their oath and starve themselves to death ? Or did a complaisant priesthood find some way whereby they could escape their self-imposed doom ? All history suggests that the latter alternative triumphed ; members of a priesthood have generally been able to find a way to save the lives of men engaged in a work for an end which would accord with their desires.

CHAPTER XIX

PAUL AND FELIX

PAUL was now a prisoner in Roman hands, and that fact saved him from the fate that would have overtaken him had the Jews been able to carry out their intention. He was kept in Herod's palace, the Praetorium of Caesarea, where he was to wait until those who had accused him came to the city, as they were instructed to do by Felix. When they arrived the case was heard.

The two men, Paul and Felix, the prisoner and the judge, presented a great contrast. Felix had been a slave ; now he owed his position as Procurator of Judea to his brother Pallas, who was a favourite minister of the Emperor Claudius. He has been described by Tacitus, a Roman historian, as a monster of lust and cruelty, who exercised the powers of a king in the spirit of a slave, and considered himself free to commit any iniquity. He was a votary of pleasure— ostentatious and extravagant. He had, however, put down the bands of robbers who had infested Palestine, and had dispersed the followers of the Egyptian whom Claudius Lysias had confounded with Paul. On the other hand, he had not hesitated to use members of the robber bands to get rid of an enemy.

The High Priest and his supporters had engaged an " orator ", or a lawyer, named Tertullus, familiar with Roman Law, to conduct the case against Paul, for now that the matter was in the hands of the Romans, the case had to be conducted on Roman principles. Like modern lawyers, Tertullus was ready to take a " brief " for either prosecution or defence, and it was quite usual for them to be employed in legal cases.

Tertullus opened the case with flattery of the judge. It might have been thought that, having regard to the character of Felix, this would not have been an easy thing to do. He took advantage of about the only point he could have used, and referred to the efforts Felix had made to put down the robbers of Palestine. Having thus created a favourable atmosphere he opened the case against Paul, whom he declared to be " a pestilent fellow, a mover of insurrections among all the Jews throughout the world, and a ringleader of the sect of the Nazarenes ".

It was a clear case of trying to arouse the prejudices of Felix by associating Paul with the insurrectionaries of the time. Developing the charge he alleged that Paul had essayed to profane the Temple. It will be noticed that the charge thus put forward differed materially from that which had been made in Jerusalem. Then it was alleged that Paul had taken Greeks into the Temple, now he had only essayed to profane the holy place. Tertullus passed over the part the Jews had taken in the tumult in the Temple court and outside, and finished by suggesting that Felix should examine Paul, and take due note of the matters laid to his charge.

The High Priest and the elders with him having endorsed this setting forth of their charges, Felix beckoned to Paul to speak in his defence. His answer was simple and effective. He spoke of the length of time Felix had been acting as judge among the Jews, a period long enough to enable him to appreciate the points he purposed to lay before him. He told him that only twelve days had passed since he entered Jerusalem. He had gone there to worship ; a fact which showed how unlikely it was that he should have been guilty of any action which would have profaned the Temple. He contended that while he had been there he had done nothing to offend the religious feelings of the Jews ; he had not disputed in the Temple, nor had he gathered a crowd, either in the Temple, in the synagogues, or in the city. He admitted that his way of worshipping the God of his fathers was regarded by the Jews as a heresy, but he added, " so serve I the God of our fathers, believing all things which are according to the Law, and which are written in the prophets ; having hope toward God, which those also themselves look for, that there shall be a resurrection both of the just and the unjust ".

It was a sober defence, and it was made even more effective as Paul proceeded to inform Felix of the special purpose for which he had come to Jerusalem. On this matter he said, " After many years I came to bring alms to my nation ". It was not to cause an offence to Jewish feelings, but to help his fellow countrymen. Having such a purpose, was it likely that he would proceed to stir up trouble ?

Then he passed on to the circumstances that led directly to the trouble. He told Felix that he had been in the Temple for the purpose of conforming to the Jewish Law in the matter of purification. Then he directly challenged the prosecution. " Let these men themselves say what wrong-doing they found when I stood before the council, except that I cried standing among them, Touching the resurrection of the dead I am called in question before you this day ".

Felix was in a quandary. No evidence had been tendered which established the guilt of the prisoner, yet he was anxious not to offend the Jews. They were a difficult people to govern, and he had to live among them. He therefore deferred the case on the ground that he wished to hear what Claudius Lysias had to say. So little impressed was he by the case that, although he committed Paul into charge, he was to be given " indulgence " (the word implies ease, liberty, or rest), and his friends were to be allowed to visit him and to minister to him.

Paul had made a favourable impression on the governor. Felix knew something of the Jews, for his wife Drusilla was a Jewess,—not a very creditable one, it is true, still she was a member of that people. She was a daughter of Herod Agrippa, and was one of the most beautiful women of the time. In her fifteenth year she had been married to the King of Emessa. Felix saw her, fell in love with her, and employed a magician of Cyprus to wean her away from her husband. The magician succeeded, and Drusilla deserted her husband and became the wife of Felix. They seem to have been a well matched pair.

Some days after the hearing of the case by Felix, he and Drusilla sat in the private part of their palace, and Paul was brought in before them. Something about the prisoner had evidently attracted Felix, for Roman governors were not usually favourable to Jews, nor were they much impressed as they listened to Jewish complaints. Perhaps Felix felt that Paul was a much better man than those who had accused him. There was another reason. Paul had said that he had visited Jerusalem to bring alms to his nation. He, or some of his friends, were evidently in control of considerable wealth, and Felix hoped it might be possible to get hold of some of it. Judging by his own experiences he thought Paul might be induced to buy his freedom, or, if he were too honourable to adopt such a course, some of his friends might do so. So Paul was sent for, and Felix and his wife listened as the Apostle spoke of the faith of Christ —the subject that Paul had so constantly spoken about at the cost of so much pain and sorrow.

On this occasion Paul took for his themes Righteousness, Temperance, and Judgment to come ; a fit trio for the pair who listened. What had Felix to do with Righteousness ? What had he to do with Self-control, the proper meaning of the word translated Temperance ? He and his wife evidently had none. As for Judgment to come, that was perhaps worse than either of the other headings. If judgment to come were a reality, and its decisions were to be based upon the actions done in this life, what hope could either of the pair have ? As Felix listened to the burning words that fell from the speaker's lips, he trembled, as well he might. Before a human judgment seat he would stand condemned on the known facts of his life ; what would the result be if he were arraigned before a Divine judgment seat such as Paul pictured ? Up to that point he and his wife had probably listened unmoved, but at the allusion to a Divine judgment, conscience intervened ; the look on Felix's face changed, he was terrified. He had heard enough. " Go thy way for the present ", he said, " when I have a convenient season, I will call unto thee."

A convenient season came ; several came ; and Felix listened to the messages that Paul spoke to him, but he listened in vain. He was evidently attracted to Paul, as some bad men are attracted at times to good men, but all the time, as he called, and recalled, Paul to his presence, there was at the back of his mind the memory that Paul had been in charge of large sums of money, and he hoped still that he might be able to obtain some of them. He hoped in vain; neither Paul, nor those who had been associated with him in the administration of the "bounty", were men of that type, so Paul remained in bonds.

There are some reasons for thinking that, somewhere about this time, Paul's financial position was greatly improved, and this may have had a part in causing Felix to continue to hope that he might be given a bribe to facilitate Paul's release. It seems that the family's property had come to him. Even if, at the time of his conversion, his father had disowned him, it was not in his power to alter the terms that governed inheritance; they were laid down in the Law. Of course, all this is conjecture, but there must have been some cause for the change in Paul's position. Not long afterwards, though a prisoner at Rome, he could hire a house for himself, and there is no further mention of working by his own hands, as he had done in the past.

Two years passed away, and Felix found himself in trouble with the Jews. Rioting broke out in the streets of Caesarea, and Roman troops were used to quell it. Then the Jews sent a deputation to Rome, where they were refused redress. Then they accused Felix of various malpractices, and this time they secured his deposition. Even then he stood in such awe of the Jews that he did what he could to please them, and when Porcius Festus was made procurator in Felix' room, he found Paul still in bonds.

CHAPTER XX

PAUL, FESTUS, AGRIPPA, BERNICE

ALTHOUGH little is known about Porcius Festus, it is clear he was a marked contrast to Felix. Josephus has only passing allusions to him, and he occupied the position of Procurator of Judea for less than two years before he died. He took his office seriously, and three days after his arrival in the province he went to Jerusalem. It was natural he should go there, for it was the chief city of the Jews, and the site of their beautiful Temple, though the object of his visit was probably to meet the leaders of the Jews, rather than to see the sights of the capital.

The two years had not lessened the hostility of the Jews to Paul, and their leaders took advantage of Festus' presence in the city to request that Paul should be brought to Jerusalem. They put forward this request, not with a desire to have his case re-heard, but because they thought it might offer an opportunity for the assassination of the prisoner on his way to the city. Festus evidently sensed their antipathy to Paul, and their intentions were again frustrated. Festus told them that Paul was in charge at Caesarea, and that he was going there shortly. " Let them therefore ", said he, " which are of power among you go down with me, and if there is anything amiss in the man, let them accuse him." Festus was a business-like man, and as soon as he had returned to Caesarea gave instructions for Paul to be brought before him. He listened to the " many and grievous complaints " which the Jews made about him, but which they completely failed to prove.

Paul's answer to the charges was simple and direct. He said, " Neither against the law of the Jews, nor against the Temple, nor against Caesar, have I sinned at all ". Festus realized that the prisoner was innocent, but with a desire to please the people over whom he had been appointed, suggested to Paul that he should go up to Jerusalem, and be judged there. Paul refused. He knew the kind of reception he was likely to get there, even if he arrived safely in the city. Past experience had shown that justice, or fair treatment, were the last things he might anticipate from the Jews. His answer was final, and it removed him out of their reach for ever.

" I stand at Caesar's judgment seat, where I ought to be judged. To the Jews have I done no wrong, as thou also very well knowest. If then I am a wrong-doer, or have committed anything worthy of death, I refuse not to die ; but if none of the things is true whereof these accuse me, no man can give me up unto them. I appeal unto Caesar ! "

There was a distinct rebuke in these words. Paul saw that Festus desired to please the Jews ; hence he asserted his privilege as a Roman citizen. By virtue of that citizenship he had a right to appeal beyond any local court to that of the Emperor himself. His claim could not be questioned, and Paul's case stood referred to Rome. Paul had taken a definite step that must lead him to Rome.

The whole incident may be regarded as an illustration of the " Ways of Providence ". When Paul was the victim of the riot in the Temple court, and was made a prisoner, there seemed little or no likelihood of reaching Rome. As a prisoner of a Roman official in Judea he was answerable to the court in that country. Owing to the anxiety of the Procurators to keep their awkward subjects quiet, he was kept in the country as a prisoner, and the hope of seeing Rome faded more and more. Yet Jesus had said to him that he must bear witness in Rome. Now the way was opened ; he must be sent to Rome.

Before Festus was able to send Paul to Caesar an incident occurred which enabled the Apostle to bear witness for Christ before some of the highest personages of the Jewish state. Agrippa, king of Iturea and Trachonitis, with his sister Bernice, came to Caesarea to salute Festus ; it was a complimentary visit on the occasion of his appointment. Agrippa was the son of the Herod who put Peter in prison, and whose terrible death is mentioned in the Acts of the Apostles. He had been king of Chalcis, and had been given the superintendence of the Temple, and the right of nominating the High Priests. Later, the kingdom of Chalcis had been exchanged for various tetrarchies, and the government of certain cities in Galilee. Agrippa has been described as " the very worst of his line "—and that is about the worst thing that could be said of anyone.

Of Bernice history relates little but evil. At the age of thirteen she was married to her uncle ; at nineteen she was a widow with two sons. Then she went to Rome where, it is said, she lived with her brother Agrippa. She afterwards married Polemo, the king of Cilicia, but she soon grew tired of him, and left him. She was a woman of remarkable beauty, like her sister Drusilla, and later became a prominent figure in the society of Rome.

The visit of Agrippa gave Festus an opportunity of consulting him concerning Paul. He would have to send a report to Rome on the prisoner, and this report must contain particulars of the charge made against him. Festus had not yet been able to do this ; in fact, it would be difficult to formulate a document that would be regarded as a satisfactory indictment by the legal authorities of Rome. Festus spoke to Agrippa of his difficulties, and arrangements were made for a further hearing of the case, at which the king should be present. No time was lost, and the next day the meeting took place in the judgment hall at Caesarea.

The occasion was marked by great pomp, for Agrippa was a king ; not a very important one then, but his kingly dignity had to be observed. In addition to Festus and Agrippa, with Bernice, there were a number of the chief captains and the principal men of the city who had been ordered to attend to add to the dignity of the occasion. The principal men of the city would wear their robes of office, and the soldiers their uniforms.

When the party had assembled Paul was brought in, wearing his prison chains. The proceedings were opened by Festus, who told Agrippa that he had found Paul in custody when he came to the city; that the Jews had tried to get him to send him to Jerusalem, but that the enquiries he had been able to make had failed to establish any real charges against him. He further told how Paul had appealed to Caesar, and must therefore be sent to him, yet, as he added, " I have no certain thing to write unto my Lord ". He finished by hoping that the day's hearing would enable him to carry out the requirements of the law.

Agrippa looked at the figure before him. Twelve years older than when he started out on his first missionary journey, Paul was still the same man. He had the same indomitable courage; the same defect of vision; the same body, only kept going by the strength of the spirit within. After a slight pause Agrippa said, " Thou art permitted to speak for thyself".

With a characteristic gesture Paul stretched out his hand, from which fetters hung, and

commenced to speak. " I think myself happy,
king Agrippa ", he said, " that I am to make my
defence before thee this day touching all things
whereof I am accused by the Jews ". He rapidly
outlined his early life, leading to the statement
that he was there " to be judged for the hope
of the promise made to the fathers ".

Suddenly he brought the matter to a focus.
" Why should it be judged incredible with you
if God raise the dead ? " Yes, why ? The Jewish
Scriptures, which Agrippa professed to believe,
contained accounts of such happenings. Elisha
had raised the dead, and the promises to the
fathers that they should possess the land, and to
David that he should have a Son who should sit
upon his throne before him, or in his presence,
involved resurrection from the dead. Such a
thing was inherent in the Jewish religion.

Then Paul resumed the summary of his life.
He told of the vision he had seen on the road to
Damascus, of the voice that came to him, the
voice of Jesus of Nazareth. He told of the way
in which he had been appointed to be " a
minister and a witness ". " Wherefore ", he
continued, " O king Agrippa, I was not dis-
obedient to the heavenly vision ". That might
be looked upon as the motto that had governed
his life ; a key to his work in endeavouring to
bring " every thought into the obedience of
Christ ". He was nearing the climax of his
address. " Having therefore obtained help of
God, I stand unto this day testifying both to

small and great, saying nothing but what the prophets and Moses did say should come ; how that Christ must suffer, and how that he first by the resurrection of the dead should proclaim light both to the people and to the Gentiles ".

Festus could not follow such strange ideas. All this talk about resurrection from the dead was absurd to him. At this point therefore, the practical Roman broke into the flow of Paul's words, saying, " Paul, thou art mad ; much learning doth turn thee unto madness ! " The energy of Paul's words had indeed made an impression upon him ; their fervour showed that the thoughts they expressed were real to Paul.

Paul stopped for a moment ; then, looking at Festus, he quietly said, " I am not mad, most excellent Festus, but speak forth words of truth and soberness ". Then, speaking to Agrippa, he continued, " The king knoweth of these things, unto whom also I speak freely, for I am persuaded that none of these things is hidden from him, for this hath not been done in a corner ".

Then he faced Agrippa, and said, " King Agrippa, believest thou the prophets ? I know that thou believest ".

Agrippa's position among the Jews must have made him acquainted with, at least, some of the things to which Paul had referred. His family had been too much mixed up with matters connected with Jesus of Nazareth for him to have been totally ignorant of them. His grandfather had ordered the babes of Bethlehem to be slain because he heard that One who was to be king of the Jews had been born. His uncle, Herod the tetrarch, had been associated with the last hours of Jesus of Nazareth, when Pilate had tried to remove responsibility from his own shoulders. In the early days of Christianity his father, Herod the king, had killed James, the brother of John, and had imprisoned Peter because he proclaimed the resurrection of Jesus. With all these points of contact which various members of his family had had with Jesus and his followers it was not possible for Agrippa to know nothing of the matters. Whatever he may have thought, he could have no idea that the things spoken of by Paul were the thoughts of a madman.

"Believest thou the Prophets?" It was a pointed question. As Superintendent of the Temple, and the nominator of the High Priests, it must be presumed he had some knowledge of the prophets; were not their writings read every Sabbath day in the assemblies of the Jews?

Agrippa was not to be caught in that way; an acceptance of the Christian position would have involved giving up too much for him. He loved position, and he loved money. In the past he had borrowed enormous sums. He therefore turned the question with a kind of jest; probably he dared not deal with it in any other way. "With but little persuasion thou wouldest fain make me out to be a Christian", he said.

There is a trace of sadness in Paul's reply. " I would to God that whether with little persuasion or with much, not only thou, but also all that hear me this day, might become such as I am ", then raising his manacled hands, he added, " except these bonds ".

Such as I am ! A short man, with a weak bodily presence, poor eyesight, a prisoner, bearing witness on his body of stripes and beatings ; a man who had been stoned, driven from town after town. " Such as I am ! " And yet, who would hesitate to choose, if choice were possible ; would he be Festus the Roman, Agrippa the Jew, Bernice the beautiful but immoral Jewess, or Paul ? There could, surely, be no hesitation, for a future is coming when three of them will be

Cast as rubbish to the void

When God hath made the pile complete, whereas Paul will be for ever associated with his Master and Lord.

The meeting was over, but little came of it. Paul's audience were convinced that the charges against him were the outcome of Jewish animosity. The leading figures of the meeting drew aside and talked the matter over. Agrippa gave expression to the result : " This man ", he said, " might have been set at liberty if he had not appealed unto Caesar ". Yes, but if he had not appealed he might never have attained his wish—" After that I must see Rome ".

CHAPTER XXI

THE VOYAGE TO ROME

FESTUS had now gathered as much information as he could concerning his prisoner, and there was nothing to prevent his sending him to Rome. A number of other prisoners were being sent in charge of a Roman centurion, and Paul was added to the company. A band of soldiers accompanied them as a guard. Paul was not alone on this journey ; the faithful Luke was with him, and Aristarchus, a Macedonian of Thessalonica who had been with Paul in Ephesus. The latter was a prisoner, for in an allusion to him in the Epistle to the Colossians, Paul speaks of him as " Aristarchus my fellow prisoner ". The company of these two men must have been a great solace to Paul, for they were tried friends.

Although the company left by a ship of Adramyttium, a town on the shore of the Aegean Sea, it was not intended to remain in it. Adramyttium was a centre of commerce, standing on the Roman road which ran between Troas and the Hellespont to the north, and to Pergamos, Ephesus and Miletus to the south, with other roads leading to a number of places ,in the interior. The centurion hoped to find a suitable ship there to take him and his prisoners to Italy.

As the ship sailed out of the harbour of Caesarea Paul took his last look at the land of his

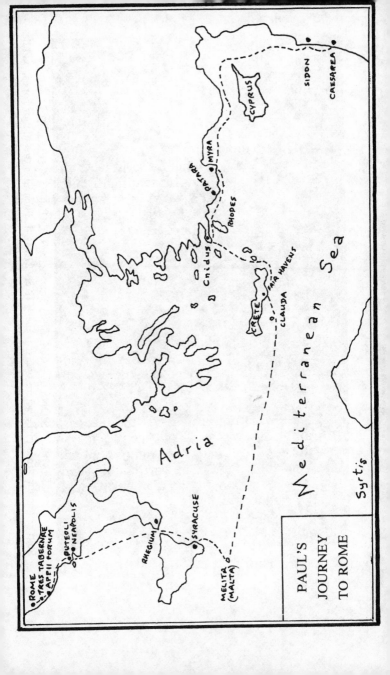

PAUL'S JOURNEY TO ROME

IMPRESSION OF PAUL'S SHIP DURING JOURNEY TO ROME

Ship at anchor "in a place where two seas met" (Acts 27:41). It illustrates the anchor ropes, paddle rudders and undergirding amidships. From *The Voyage and Shipwreck of Paul*, by James Smith

ancestors, whose inhabitants had treated him so cruelly, but of whom he had written, " My heart's desire, and my supplication to God, is for them, that they might be saved ". This feeling must have been very keen as he saw the coastline of Palestine gradually fade away in the distance, but, though a prisoner, he probably consoled himself that he was on the way to the heart of the Empire—Rome.

The day following their departure the ship called at Sidon. In the short time Paul had been in the charge of the centurion, he had impressed him so favourably that he permitted him to visit his friends and " refresh " himself. The Greek really implies something of a more active character than the English word may suggest ; it could be read, "that he might avail himself of their care".

As soon as the voyage was resumed difficulties commenced. Ordinarily ships making such a journey would have sailed direct to Myra, keeping Cyprus on their right hand, but on this journey the winds were contrary, and the ship had to go slowly by the coasts of Cilicia and Pamphilia, where the mariners were able to take advantage of the land breezes, and of the current which there runs steadily westward. This course avoided the open waters of the Mediterranean. It was a slow journey as, according to one early manuscript, fifteen days were occupied in passing along the Pamphilian coast.

When they arrived at Myra, on the south coast of Asia Minor, they found a ship of

Alexandria, loaded with corn for the people of Rome. In those days Egypt was one of the granaries of Rome, and a regular line of communications was kept up so that the corn of Egypt might be brought to Rome to supply its teeming population with food. The ships were large, and usually sailed direct from Alexandria to Puteoli ; probably this one had been driven out of its course by stress of weather, or it may have called at Myra to discharge some part of its cargo, as Myra is referred to in an inscription as a horrea, that is storehouse, of corn. An opportunity to sail in such a ship was not be missed, and the centurion transferred the prisoners to it.

The winds remained contrary and the progress continued to be slow. After sailing many days they reached Cnidus, a hundred and twenty miles, or thereabouts, from Myra. That many days should have been taken to cover such a distance shows the difficulties they encountered. Here it was necessary to make a decision as to their further course. They could put into Cnidus, or they could make for Crete. They chose the latter course, which meant that they had to leave the protection of the land. They could not sail against the wind, so they turned southward, and sought the shelter afforded by the Isle of Crete. With difficulty the eastern end of the island was rounded, and they reached a place known as Fair Havens. Here for a time they stayed, a stay that covered the Jewish Day of Atonement, which indicated that the journey

was being made in the autumn when gales were
to be expected.

At this time of the year sailing was dangerous
for the ships of those days ; in fact, all navigation
on the open sea was usually discontinued by that
time. The outlook was getting serious, and a
council was held to decide what should be done.
Paul had had considerable experience of the sea,
and knew what being shipwrecked meant (see the
Foreword), and advised that they should remain
where they were, for a time, otherwise they would
risk both ship and cargo, to say nothing of their
lives. The ship being on government service,
the decision rested with the centurion, who, not
unnaturally, paid more attention to the advice
of the Master of the ship than to a prisoner. His
advice was that as the harbour of Fair Havens
was not a convenient one, they should endeavour
to reach Phenice, further along the coast, which
was better protected than Fair Havens.

Taking advantage of a change of wind,
when a south wind blew softly, they left Fair
Havens, hoping, no doubt, to be able to finish
their voyage and reach Puteoli. The fair
prospect that had encouraged them soon passed.
A great eddying wind coming from the mountains
of Crete, away to the north-east, struck the ship.
A modern ship's captain, talking of his own
experiences has said, " The wind comes down
from those mountains fit to blow the ship out of
the water "[1]. In the Acts the wind is spoken

---

[1]Ramsay ; *Paul, Traveller and Roman Citizen*, p. 327.

of as " tempestuous " (Gk. typhonic), and is called Euroquilo. For the ships that sailed over those waters in the First Century, A.D., such a wind was even worse than it is today. As soon as it caught the ship, the Master and his crew were helpless ; they " gave way " to the gale, and the ship was " driven ".

Matters soon became desperate. The ship was driven past the island of Clauda, south of Crete, where for a short time they found a little protection. They took advantage of this to take what steps they could to increase their chances of weathering the storm. The boat, which had been towed behind during the short spell of easier weather, was dragged into the ship. Paul and his companions took part in this task, as Luke speaks of " we ", and records that it was done with difficulty. Then some of the timbers of the ship began to break away, and the crew had to undergird the ship, passing a strong cable round it, under the keel and across the deck, to prevent other timbers starting.

By this time another danger faced them. The wind, still blowing from the north-east, was driving them towards the coast of Africa, and had they continued travelling in that direction they would have reached the great quicksands off the North African coast known as the Syrtis. They were still some distance away, but they would inevitably reach them if they continued in the same direction. They therefore " lowered the gear ", thus lessening the amount of sail, so that it might modify their course. After they had done this they continued to drive, but in a different direction. Still the storm continued to rage, and the waves threatened to overwhelm the ship. In the circumstances the only thing they could do was to lighten the ship so that it might ride higher on the waves. They threw some of the cargo overboard ; then the tackling of the ship, doing so " with our own hands ", as Luke puts it. There seemed to be nothing more they could do, and the gale continued with unabated force. Day after day passed, and neither sun, moon, nor stars could be seen, so that they had no means of knowing either where they were, or in what direction they were really going. Of course there was no mariner's compass in those days.

In this crisis Paul showed the manner of man he was. In the storm, and amid the labour involved in their efforts to save the ship, the sailors and others had found no time, or opportunity, to get any proper meals. Now Paul spoke to them. He reminded them of the advice he had given at Fair Havens. " But ", he continued, " I exhort you to be of good cheer ; for there shall be no loss of life among you, but only of the ship. For this night an angel of the God, whose I am, whom I serve, stood before me, saying, Fear thou not, Paul ; thou must stand before Caesar ; and, lo, God hath granted thee all them that sail with thee. Wherefore, be of good cheer, men, for I believe God, that it shall be even as it hath been spoken unto me. Howbeit we must be cast upon a certain island ".

The strength, or the weakness, of a man is best shown by his reactions in a time of crisis. By this criterion Paul was a truly great man. Picture the scene. A ship out of control, tossing helplessly on the waves. Every hope of bringing it safely to port has been given up. The mariners are hungry and tired, worn out with their exertions. In their midst stands a little Jew, poor in bodily presence, yet with the tossing waves all round the ship, and the winds howling, he can calmly say, " I BELIEVE GOD ", and " there shall be no loss of any man's life among you ". It is an example of transcendent faith. Might not the appearance of the angel have been but a dream ? Paul knew it was real ; God had sent His messenger. His confidence allayed the fears of his fellow voyagers, and they partook of a necessary meal, one that helped them to face whatever was coming.

Fourteen days after leaving Fair Havens, as they were still drifting, the sound of breaking waves was heard. It was about midnight, and though nothing could be seen, the sound told the sailors that they were nearing land. Soundings were immediately taken, and they found they were in twenty fathoms of water ; a little later it was fifteen fathoms. They were rapidly approaching land, and the breakers indicated that it was a rocky coast. They at once cast out four anchors from the stern, " and wished for the day " ! Anchoring by the stern was unusual, but in the circumstances it was the only thing to do. Had they anchored from the bow, the ship would have swung round, and have been much harder to handle when dawn broke.

Lying thus at anchor near to land, the sailors attempted to leave the ship and secure their own safety by using the boat, which they had lowered. Their purpose was frustrated by Paul, who stands out, not only as the calmest, but also the most vigilant, man on board. His intervention caused the soldiers to cut the ropes, and the boat drifted away.

The critical time would come in the morning, and it was necessary for crew and passengers to be prepared for it. Paul therefore besought them to partake of food, and, in the presence of all, gave thanks for it. His cheerfulness was infectious, and the courage of all on board was increased by his words and example.

With the energy supplied by the food they had eaten, the crew and others further lightened the ship by casting all the corn into the sea. As the light increased they saw the land before them through the mist, for it was still raining, but none of them could recognize it. As there was a bay with a beach they cut away the anchors, and hoisted the foresail, and so let the ship drive toward the shore. As the wind caught her she gathered speed and sped forward until she struck a sandbank in the middle of the bay. There she stayed, but as the stern was buffeted by the waves it began to break up. The soldiers suggested that the prisoners should be killed in case they attempted to escape ; for if they had, Roman discipline would have held the soldiers responsible for it. By the centurion's intervention they were prevented from carrying out their suggestion, and so, by swimming, or availing themselves of floating wreckage, all got safely to land.

Their lot was still an evil one. Wet through by immersion in the sea, exposed to the rain that was still falling, they must have appreciated to the full the hospitality shown to them by the natives of the island. They found that they were in Melita, the modern Malta. It might be thought that mariners accustomed to navigate the Mediterranean would have recognized the island, but the spot where they had been wrecked, now known as St. Paul's Bay, lies right away from the part of the island usually seen.

The first thing wanted by the shipwrecked company was warmth, and a fire was at once kindled. Paul, with characteristic energy, took part in collecting the materials for the fire. As he did so a viper fastened itself on his hand. The natives at once concluded that he must be a bad criminal, and that, though he had escaped from death by drowning, he could not evade it by other means. Paul shook off the reptile into the fire, and when the people of the island looked on and saw no evil following they changed their ideas, and concluded that he must be a god.

In due course Paul and his company were received by the chief man of the island, who entertained them for three days. His father was ill, suffering from fever and dysentery. Paul went to the sick man, prayed for power to heal, and laid his hands on him, and the man recovered. News of what had happened quickly spread through the island, and many others who suffered from various diseases came and were cured.

The party remained in the island for three months, at the end of which time, with the reopening of the Mediterranean for navigation, they were able to resume their journey towards Rome, bearing with them many tokens of the appreciation of the islanders. They took passage in another ship of Alexandria which had wintered in the island, and was then ready to sail for Italy. The voyage was favourable. They landed first at Syracuse on the east coast of Sicily, where they stayed for three days ; then they made for the mainland, calling at Rhegium. With a change of wind, which commenced to blow from the south, progress was rapid, and the next day they reached Puteoli ; they had covered a distance of a hundred and eighty miles. Little is recorded of their stay here, but that little is suggestive. " We found brethren, and were desired to tarry with them seven days." It must have been a cheering incident to the Apostle and his two companions. Months had elapsed since they left Caesarea, and the sight and company of other members of the household of faith, even if not known to them personally, must have been most welcome.

At the end of the seven days, during which there would be an opportunity to take part in a meeting for the Breaking of Bread, they renewed the journey to Rome.

The seven days at Puteoli gave time for news to reach Rome of the approach of Paul. Some knew him personally, and there were many to whom he had sent greetings in his letter to the brethren there. He had told them in that letter that he hoped to meet them, and now he was on the way—nearing the city ! That he was coming as a prisoner would naturally be a disappointment to them, but it probably made them all the more desirous of showing their appreciation and sympathy. Quite a number journeyed to greet him. One party met him at the Market of Appius, and another at a place called the Three Taverns. The former place was some forty-three miles from Rome, and the other about thirty-three.

Paul seems to have been rather depressed as he journeyed toward Rome. Perhaps during the week he had spent at Puteoli he had heard something of the cruelties and enormities of the Emperor Nero, to whom he had appealed, and who was to decide his fate. But when he met the brethren " he thanked God and took courage ".

CHAPTER XXII

PAUL IN ROME

OF the events that took place during the two years Paul spent in Rome we know very little. On his arrival he would be handed over to the chief of the Imperial police, with a statement setting out the charges against him, and any comments that Festus may have made upon the case. These, and the report of the centurion, would ensure Paul being given the best treatment that could be accorded to a prisoner.

The records in the Acts of the Apostles give a very brief account of the period, and say nothing at all about his appearance before Caesar's court, but Paul's letters, written during his imprisonment, enable certain details to be filled in.

Although a prisoner, guarded by a Roman soldier, he was allowed to dwell in a house which he hired, and in which he could receive visits from his friends and others, and carry out his great work of proclaiming the gospel. His old friends Aquila and Priscilla had been able to return to Rome, and their house was one of the places used as a meeting place for the Christians of the city. They, and others who are referred to in the salutations at the end of the epistle to the Romans, some of whom were Paul's kinsmen, were able to visit him, and by their love and sympathy cheer his captivity. The one drawback was the constant presence of a Roman soldier to whom he was chained, and though the chain might be a light one, such company could hardly be congenial to a man of Paul's temperament. A Roman soldier's training and temperament did not tend to bring out the higher qualities, and some were coarse and brutal. No doubt Paul accepted the position and made the best of it. As will be seen later, some of these soldiers were of a better type, or they became so.

Still acting on the principle of " to the Jew first ", Paul's first efforts were directed towards his kinsmen according to the flesh. Three days after his arrival in the city he sent for the chief men among the Jews, and told them of the circumstances that had brought him to Rome. " Brethren ", he said, " though I had done nothing against the people, or the customs of our fathers, I was delivered prisoner from Jerusalem into the hands of the Romans, who, when they had examined me, desired to set me at liberty, because there was no cause of death in me. But when the Jews spoke against it, I was constrained to appeal unto Caesar ; not that I had ought to accuse my nation of. For this cause therefore did I entreat you to see and to speak with me : because that for the hope of Israel I am bound with this chain ".

Apparently the Jews of the Capital knew little about him ; they were therefore ready to listen to what he had to say. On the other hand,

they knew something of his " sect ", and said it
was everywhere spoken against. In the end an
appointment was made for a meeting to be held
in his house, so that he might explain what this
" sect " stood for. Many came, and to them
he expounded the matter, testifying the Kingdom
of God, persuading them concerning Jesus, both
from the Law of Moses, and from the prophets.

How earnest he was in this matter may be
gathered from the fact that he continued doing
so for the whole of a day—from morning to
evening. It was characteristic of him ; it was
Troas over again, only with a different kind of
audience. As he referred to testimony after
testimony from the Old Testament he was lost
in his theme ; nothing else mattered. As he
proceeded, however, mutterings could be heard
among his audience ; then the mutterings turned
to interruptions, and finally to wranglings,
amongst his visitors.

Just before the meeting broke up Paul
reminded them of some sayings of their prophets
which were not at all complimentary to their
race, and finished up with some words of his
own, " Be it known unto you that this salvation
of God is sent unto the Gentiles ; they will also
hear ".

What result followed we do not know. Did
some believe and come again ? Some did, no
doubt, though these were probably but a few.
On the other hand the Gentiles did hear, and
during the time he remained in Rome he spoke

to all who came to the house of the unsearchable riches of Christ.

At this point Luke finishes his history; the rest must be gathered from Paul's letters, a little perhaps from tradition, though the latter must be treated with reserve.

The delays of the law, and may be the disinclination of Nero to be bothered with the affairs of one whom he probably thought of as " a little Jew ", caused two years to pass. During that time Paul's constant contact with members of the Praetorian Guard brought the knowledge of Christ to some of them. He refers to them in one of the letters he wrote while he was in Rome, in which he says, " My bonds became manifest in Christ throughout the whole praetorian guard ". In the conclusion of that epistle he wrote, " All the saints salute you, especially they that are of Caesar's household ". Such passages suggest an active life, even though he was a prisoner.

Of course he was not alone; Timothy was with him during part of the time; so was Luke. Others who are mentioned include Aristarchus, Tychicus, Epaphroditus, Demas, and Onesimus.

The mention of Onesimus introduces a pleasing picture of Paul's work in Rome. Rome was a city of contrasts; it had its very wealthy, its proud patricians, and its very poor. Morally it might be described as, in some parts, a sink of iniquity; the first chapter of the letter to the Romans is a sufficient evidence of this. In such a

" sink " a runaway slave, for that is what Onesimus was, might hope to avoid recapture. Onesimus had run away from his master, Philemon of Colosse, and had, presumably, taken some of his master's property with him, thereby belying his name, for Onesimus means profitable. How he came to meet Paul we do not know. It may be that as his late master was a Christian, his conduct had impressed the slave. Perhaps in Rome he remembered various acts of Philemon. Probably he had attended a meeting held by some of the Christians of Rome. Whatever the means, he came into contact with Paul ; his heart was touched ; he believed and was baptized.

The conversion of a runaway slave does not seem to have been much of an achievement for a man who had done as much as Paul, yet it led to one of the most beautiful epistles in the New Testament being written. Paul loved the runaway, but by the law of the times Onesimus was the property of Philemon, and he must go back. Paul had written before this, " Wast thou called being a bondservant, care not for it " ; so he sent Onesimus back to his master with a letter, and the letter was an example of what a fraternal letter may be.

Paul did not write as an Apostle, as he usually did, and as he did in the letter which Onesimus carried to the Church in Colosse. He wrote as " the prisoner of Jesus Christ ", and he besought Philemon on behalf of Onesimus, whom, as he said, he had begotten in his bonds, and had sent back in the hope that Philemon would receive him, " no longer as a servant (i.e. a slave), but more than a servant, a brother beloved ". Note the delicate way in which Paul expressed himself. " If then thou countest me a partner, receive him as myself. But if he hath wronged thee at all, or oweth thee ought, put that on mine account ; I, Paul, write it with mine own hand, I will repay it . . . Yea, brother, let me have joy of thee in the Lord ; refresh my heart in Christ."

Before you read further, read that letter as it appears in the Bible ; it is exquisitely expressed, and makes delightful reading.

With the letter to Philemon another was sent, addressed to the Church in Colosse. Epaphras, who was connected with the Colossian ecclesia, was then in Rome, a fellow prisoner, and a " beloved fellow servant ". He told Paul the circumstances of the Church. Whilst there was much to be thankful for, there were things that needed to be rectified. So Paul wrote a letter to the Church, taking advantage of the return of Onesimus and Tychicus. Looking through this epistle, and others written at the same time, it will be seen that the tendency to error had increased, and that error had grown more plausible. In the past the main trouble had been caused by Jewish Christians attempting to impose the obligations of the Jewish Law upon Gentile converts. These attempts had never been completely stopped ; they still continued, but the

VIA APPIA: The Appian Way
Last stage of Paul's journey to Rome

PAUL THE ORATOR: The Apostle, with arm outstretched,
on the column of Marcus in modern Rome

principal trouble now was "philosophy and vain deceit ".

In view of the philosophic speculations that were prevalent, the epistle to the Colossians is largely a declaration of the truth concerning Christ in his relation to God, and his place in the Divine plan of redemption. It shows the erroneous character of the teaching of the Gentile philosophers. Paul speaks of Christ as "the image of the invisible God, the firstborn of all creation ", a statement which in opposition to the teachings of the philosophers, prepares the minds for the reception of the more satisfying doctrine of God-manifestion. The acceptance of the doctrine prepares the mind so that it may rise to an appreciation of the "riches of the full assurance of understanding, that they might know the mystery of God, even Christ ". In such things lies the explanation of a number of "hard sayings" in this, and other epistles written about the same time. Their meaning is not usually on the surface, and must be gained by a study of the sayings of Paul, and by reference to the books which throw light on such subjects.

To give even an outline of the matters spoken of in this epistle would occupy much space, so one or two extracts must suffice. Here is one example. "Having been buried with him (Christ) in baptism, wherein ye were also raised with him through faith in the working of God." Here a death, a burial, and a resurrection are symbolically expressed in the act of baptism.

There could be no better illustration of what baptism really is—a burial in water, whereby one dies to the past, and rises with Christ to " newness of life ". To those who realize this there is tremendous meaning in the words that follow. " If then ye were raised together with Christ, seek the things that are above." " Put on therefore, as God's elect, holy and beloved, a heart of compassion, kindness, humility, meekness, longsuffering, forbearing one another, and forgiving each other . . . even as Christ forgave you, so also do ye."

Paul did not confine his attention to great thoughts such as those mentioned ; he got down also to the humdrum things of life, as many would consider them. He speaks of the varying duties of husbands and wives, children and fathers, servants and masters. The contrast is startling ; here are some of the sublimest thoughts about God and Christ side by side with the everyday duties of the common life of human beings. In any but the greatest of men a sudden change like that would make the letter lose much of its force, but not with Paul ; he was too versatile to be humdrum.

Tychicus was the bearer of another letter, the Epistle to the Ephesians, which was written at the same time. It is generally agreed that this letter was not sent to the Church in Ephesus only, but was a kind of circular letter sent to various Churches. In one of the great manuscripts its destination is left blank, and it will be noticed

that, unlike other epistles, it contains no messages
or salutations to individuals, though Paul had
lived in Ephesus for a comparatively long time,
and must have known many Christians there.

This epistle has an outline of the Christian
faith, which is set forth as a sevenfold unity ;
the unity of the Spirit which is to be held in the
bonds of peace. That unity is thus defined.
" One body, and one Spirit, even as also ye were
called in the one hope of your calling ; one
Lord, one faith, one baptism, one God and
Father of all, who is over all, and through all, and
in all." In this unity Jews and Gentiles were
to be included, for he speaks of some who were
at one time afar off, separate from Christ,
alienated from the commonwealth of Israel,
but are now made near in the blood of Christ.

As in the letter to the Colossians allusions
to deeper things are found side by side with
allusions to the daily duties of those who stand
in various relationships to one another, but
in this letter the two aspects are brought into
close association with each other, for, having
spoken of the duty of husbands loving their wives,
Paul goes on to say, " even as Christ loved the
Church, and gave himself up for it ; that he
might sanctify it, having cleansed it by the
washing of water with the word, that he might
present the Church to himself, a glorious Church,
not having spot, or wrinkle, or any such thing,
but that it should be holy and without blame ".
What ordinary writer would have thought of

turning marriage relationships and duties into an occasion for such a theme ?

Just one more extract may be given from this epistle ; note the beauty of thought and expression : " Be ye kind one to another, tender-hearted, forgiving each other, even as God also in Christ, forgave you ". Like all Paul's letters it must be read to be properly appreciated, and it should be read through at one sitting.

During the time Paul was at Rome Epaphroditus arrived from Philippi with a further gift to Paul from the Church in that city. No other Church seems to have acted in that way, though the Philippians had " once and again " ministered to his necessities. This time Paul was able to say, " I have all things and abound ; I am filled ; having received from Epaphroditus the things that came from you, an odour of a sweet smell, a sacrifice acceptable, well pleasing to God ". " I have all things and abound " ! Remember, the man who wrote those words was a prisoner, chained to a Roman soldier ! Yet in that same letter, Paul wrote, " I rejoice, yea, and will rejoice ". " Rejoice in the Lord " ; " Rejoice in the Lord alway ; again I will say, Rejoice " ; " I rejoice in the Lord greatly ". The man who could write in that way, and in such circumstances, was one who could rise completely above his circumstances, and see the goodness of God in everything.

In the letter Paul tells of some of the things that helped him to rejoice in his troubles. Here are his own words. " Now I would have you know, brethren, that the things which happened unto me have fallen out rather unto the progress of the gospel ; so that my bonds became manifest in Christ throughout the whole praetorian guard, and to all the rest ; and that most of the brethren in the Lord, being confident through my bonds, are more abundantly bold to speak the word of God without fear." Even members of Caesar's household heard his words, and became members of the Christian community.

One of the matters dealt with in this letter, which may be mentioned here, is that which deals with the power of thought. He wrote, " Finally, brethren, whatsoever things are honourable, whatsoever things are just, whatsoever things are true, whatsoever things are pure, whatsoever things are lovely, whatsoever things are of good report ; if there be any virtue, and if there be any praise, *think on these things . . .* " Always remember that thoughts lead to words and deeds. As a man thinketh, so is he.

In the ways mentioned in this chapter, speaking to those who came to his house ; writing letters to various Churches (at least one other was written besides those mentioned—one to the Church in Laodicea), sending and receiving messengers to and from various Churches—two years passed away. Altogether Paul spent four years in captivity ; two in Caesarea and two in Rome. Why was there so much delay ? No definite answer can be given. Documents may have been lost in the shipwreck. His accusers may have wasted time ; knowing that their case was hopeless, they may have adopted this expedient to keep Paul in prison as long as possible.

There is no need to feel that these were wasted years. Whatever hardships may have been involved, they had one inestimable advantage ; they gave Paul time to think. In the past there had been so much movement, so many people to see and to speak to about Christ crucified and the Kingdom of God. Speaking, persuading, travelling ; his time had been fully occupied. Now, in captivity, he had time to think and if one would appreciate the value of that opportunity, he should read the epistles referred to in this chapter once again. In one sense we may well thank God for those years of quiet, though to Paul they may have seemed very hard and very long.

No record has been preserved of the trial that followed, and it would be useless to speculate upon what happened. All that can be said is that the proceedings ended in a verdict of Not Guilty, and Paul was once again a free man, with freedom to worship as a Christian. The prayers of the brethren for which he had asked had been offered up, and had ascended before the throne of God, and His servant was, for a time, given an opportunity to finish his work.

CHAPTER XXIII

THE FINISHED COURSE

WITH his renewed freedom Paul entered upon the last phase of his life, though, unfortunately, very little is known of the events that took place during that time. Questions crowd upon the mind. Where did he go? What did he do? The answers can only be gathered from scattered hints in the letters he wrote. It is most likely that he first journeyed eastward, visiting his brethren in the faith in the Churches he had established during his previous travels, carrying out his policy of strengthening the disciples. He certainly intended to visit the Christians in Philippi, for he had written, " But I hope in the Lord Jesus to send Timothy shortly unto you, that I also may be of good comfort when I know your state, . . . Him, therefore, I hope to send at once, so soon as I shall see how it will go with me, but I am persuaded in the Lord that I myself also shall come shortly ". In the little letter he had written about Onesimus he had asked Philemon of Colosse to prepare him a lodging. Visits to Philippi and Colosse would be likely to lead him to other places, such as Corinth and Thessalonica, also to Ephesus. His words suggest that he had something of this in mind, for he wrote to Timothy, " As I exhorted thee to tarry at Ephesus when I was going into Macedonia . . . " He certainly visited Crete, for he left Titus there to set things in order, and to appoint elders in the Church. His journeyings took him to Miletus and Nicopolis. Tradition, following his expressed hope, says that he journeyed as far as Spain. The tradition is a very early one, and may be correct.

It is impossible to fix the order of his journeys covering these places, and it must suffice just to mention them, and glean the rest from his epistles.

The fact that his letters mention these places in such a way shows that he returned to his old life of service. To him still, to live was Christ, and the work had to be carried on. Yet there was a change. Whatever work he may have done in preaching, he was concerned about the organization of the Churches he had established. His letters of the period, those to Timothy and Titus, are largely taken up with this matter, and to combating certain heresies that had crept into the Christian communities.

In the first epistle to Timothy, and that to Titus, evidences of the latter are clearly seen. The heresy was called Gnosticism—a word which means " knowledge "—because those who held these ideas claimed special knowledge. This which had been working at an earlier stage, had grown, and its advocates had become bolder. In Asia Minor and Crete gnosticism was strong, owing probably to the semi-Oriental character of the peoples of those places. It was for this reason he left Timothy and Titus in Ephesus and Crete respectively. Timothy was in Ephesus that he might charge certain men " not to teach a different doctrine, neither to give heed to fables and endless genealogies ". Titus in Crete was to " set in order the things that were wanting ". " Profane babblings (the word rather suggests empty sounding and fruitless discussion) and oppositions of the knowledge (*gnosis*) which is falsely so-called " were among the things that he was to put down.

The three epistles referred to are the only contemporary evidence of what was happening ; at the same time they give at least some indication of Paul's last few years. From them we can see the nature of the change that had taken place. Some had " turned aside unto vain talking, desiring to be teachers of the Law, though they understood not what they said, nor whereof they confidently affirmed ". Paul names Hymenaeus and Alexander, who, he said, had made shipwreck concerning the faith. He refers to " profane and old wives' fables " which were being taught by some. There was among them a " love of money ", which he said was a root of all kinds of evil.

It will be seen that it was not a light task that Paul imposed upon Timothy and Titus. They were exhorted to be examples to the members of the Churches to which they had been sent ; a difficult task at the best of times.

One of the principal topics in the letters sent to them was that of the qualifications men should possess for the offices of bishops and deacons. An exceedingly high standard is set before candidates for either of these offices. Bishops were to be irreproachable, the husbands of one wife, temperate (i.e. they were to exercise self-control), soberminded, orderly, given to hospitality, apt to teach, not brawlers, not quarrelsome over wine, not strikers, but gentle, not contentious, not lovers of money ; able to rule their own families ; exercising control of their children. They were not to be novices, that is, inexperienced, nor puffed up, and, moreover, they must have a good report from those who were without. A combination of these characteristics is not often found, and the mere enumeration of them shows how important Paul considered this office to be. Such men are rare. They may be known by various titles, bishops, elders, presiding brethren, according to the custom of the community in which they officiate ; but these are the characteristics they should have.

Scarcely less important were the qualifications which Paul laid down for those who acted as deacons, that is, servants, for the Greek means servants, servants of the Church. They were to be grave, not double-tongued, not given to much wine, nor greedy of filthy lucre, and they must hold the mystery of the faith in a pure conscience. However much the circumstances may have changed during the centuries since these instructions were given, these qualifications still apply.

There is much in these letters about a number of matters that are sure to arise in any organization. They are not dealt with here, but, as in the case of the other letters, the epistles should be given careful consideration so that their meaning may be ascertained.

The freedom which Paul enjoyed after his " appeal to Caesar " does not seem to have lasted long ; then a further charge was made against him. During the interval between the two imprisonments, a complete change took place in the attitude of the Emperors to the Christians and the Christian religion. It probably coincided with Nero's attempt to transfer the responsibility for the fire that destroyed much of Rome from himself to the Christians.

In the persecution which followed Paul was arrested and put in prison. On the previous occasion he had been permitted to dwell in his own hired house ; this time there was no such consideration. Everything seemed to be against the aged Apostle. In the last letter he wrote he said, " Only Luke (the faithful Luke, the beloved physician) is with me ". Friends like Demas had forsaken him, " having loved the present world ". The Christians of Asia had turned against him, and his few faithful friends were away on various missions.

Something of his condition may be gathered from the request he made that Timothy should

come to Rome. " Do thy diligence ", Paul wrote,
" to come shortly unto me . . . The cloak that
I left at Troas with Carpus, bring when thou
comest, and the books, especially the parchments." The words picture an aged man, worn
out by the experiences of a life full of hardships,
difficulties of travel, persecutions, beatings, ship-
wrecks, and anxious for the welfare of others, now
in a cold and probably damp prison, longing for
a cloak to keep him warm.

What were the parchments, one wonders?
Were they legal documents? Something to
vindicate his claim to Roman citizenship? Or
portions of the ancient Jewish Scriptures? What
could be better calculated to cheer the aged
prisoner than some of the Psalms, or the glowing
pictures of the Prophets? They would take his
mind from his own troubles to the troubles,
and the deliverances, of others, to a contemplation of God as his Rock and Fortress, his Strong
Tower and his Deliverer. The cloak, the books
and the parchments are allusions that throw
light on Paul's experiences during his last
days.

At the first hearing of this trial he was
quite alone ; " no one took my part ", he sorrowfully wrote, " but all forsook me ; may it not be
laid to their account ". Yet he was not alone.
Christ had told his disciples, " Lo, I am with
you alway, even unto the end of the age ".
Paul knew of this promise, and realized its fulfil-
ment in his own case, for he continued, " Never-

theless the Lord stood by me and strengthened me ". In the power given to him by the presence of his Master, he was once more able to proclaim his message to all who were assembled in the court. For the moment he was saved ; he was " delivered out of the mouth of the lion ". But he was not free, for he had to face yet another charge before his judges ; and Paul had no doubt what the result would be.

It was during the brief interval that separated the " first hearing " and the final trial, Paul wrote the Second Letter to Timothy. Timothy was far away, and Paul desired to see him again, and to be cheered by his company. He knew that death was not far off ; what were his thoughts ? Some of them are suggested by the things he wrote, for they are self-revealing. " Paul, an apostle of Christ Jesus, by the will of God, according to the promise of life which is in Jesus Christ." " Christ Jesus hath abolished death, and brought life and incorruption to light through the gospel." " I am persuaded that he is able to guard that which I have committed unto him against that day." " If we died with him, we shall also live with him." Thus with death a certainty, he knew the promise of life, of reigning with Christ, of Christ's appearing and Kingdom, the crown of righteousness that was laid up for him, and was to be given to all those who loved the Master's appearing.

Thoughts such as these carried him beyond the troubled present, and his approaching death,

to the joy that was to be his in the age to come
and the Kingdom of God.

Amid the troubles that were closing in upon
him there were comforts and consolations. Did
the Christians of Asia turn away from him ?
there was one Onesiphorus, who diligently
sought through the city of Rome till he found
him, and refreshed him. " He was not ashamed
of my chain ", Paul wrote. Then there was
John Mark. He had left Paul in the past under
circumstances that hurt Paul. Now the old
man longed for him ; he was " profitable for the
ministry". Aquila and Priscilla were still
among his friends, though evidently far away,
for he sends his greetings to them in the end of
this last letter. There were others also who
joined in these salutations.

In this last letter, giving the latest thoughts
of the Apostle, there are a number of exhortations
that deserve to be specially noted. " Hold the
pattern of sound words which thou hast heard
from me, in faith and love which is in Christ
Jesus." " The things which thou hast heard
from me commit thou to faithful men, who are
competent to teach others also." " Shun profane
babblings." " Foolish and ignorant questions
refuse, knowing that they gender strifes."

In this last letter, too, Paul gave a direct
testimonial to the Scriptures. The whole passage
is worthy of reproduction. "Abide thou in the
things which thou hast learned and hast been
assured of, knowing of whom thou hast learned

them ; and that from a babe thou hast known the sacred writings, which are able to make thee wise unto salvation through faith which is in Christ Jesus. All Scripture is given by inspiration of God (A.V.) and is also profitable for teaching, for reproof, for correction, for instruction in righteousness, that the man of God may be complete, furnished completely unto every good work."

Whether Timothy and Mark arrived in Rome in time to see their beloved master and comrade once more is not known. There is a complete veil over the last days of Paul ; even tradition tells only of his death. As a Roman citizen he was saved from the cruel and revolting forms in which death overtook many of his fellow believers under the persecution of Nero. Let a Roman historian tell what those ways were.

"They died in torments, and their torments were embittered by insult and derision. Some were nailed to crosses ; others were sewn up in the skins of wild beasts and exposed to the fury of dogs ; others again were smeared over with combustible materials, and used as torches to illuminate the darkness of the night. The gardens of Nero were destined for the melancholy spectacle, and the Emperor mingled with the populace in the dress and attitude of a charioteer."

From such horrible forms of death Paul was spared, and, somewhere outside the walls of

Rome, he met his death by the executioner's sword. The actual spot where it took place matters little. In his last letter he had written,

I have fought the good fight,
I have finished the course,
I have kept the faith.

Now his work was done; the faith had been proclaimed from Jerusalem to Rome, and may be even further west; and the old man, aged beyond his years, fell asleep. His life, and his death, illustrate what he meant when he wrote, "For me to live is Christ, and to die is gain". Ever since the day when the light streamed about him on the road to Damascus, Paul had lived for Christ. His own words best describe that life. "I have been crucified with Christ; yet I live; and yet no longer I, but Christ liveth in me; and that life which I now live in the flesh I live in faith, the faith which is in the Son of God, who loved me, and gave himself up for me." In that life he bore about in the body the dying of Jesus, that "the life also of Jesus may be manifested in his body".

To him, death was gain. The crucifying was over, and he sleeps in Jesus until the time comes for him to realize his life's aim, and be "for ever with the Lord".